Darwin's Odyssey

THE VOYAGE OF THE BEAGLE

Darwin's Odyssey

THE VOYAGE OF THE BEAGLE

KEVIN JACKSON

London and New York

Darwin's Odyssey
The Voyage of the Beagle
9 8 7 6 5 4 3 2 1

First published by TSB, 2020

Published in 2021 in the United States by
Leapfrog Press Inc.
P.O. Box 1293
Dunkirk, New York 14048

Distributed in the United States by
Consortium Book Sales and Distribution
St. Paul, Minnesota 55114
www.cbsd.com

© Kevin Jackson, 2020
Author portrait: © Marzena Pogorzały
www.marzenapogorzaly.com

Cover, text and map design: James Shannon
Set in Adobe Garamond Pro and 1689 GLC Garamond Pro

ISBN: 978-1-948585-17-0 (paperback)

Printed and bound in the United Kingdom by TJ Books Ltd

About the Author – Kevin Jackson

Kevin Jackson was an English writer, broadcaster and film-maker. He had also been a Teaching Fellow of Vanderbilt University, Nashville; a radio producer and television director for the BBC; Associate Arts Editor for *The Independent* and a roving reporter for *Night and Day* Magazine, where his assignments included a week on a fishing boat in Atlantic waters, a training mission on a Royal Navy aircraft carrier and a helicopter flight to an oil rig in the Caspian, near Baku. His books include *Constellation of Genius* (Hutchinson), a history of modernism which was a Book of the Week in *The Guardian* and a Book of the Year in the *Express*; *Invisible Forms* (Picador); *Carnal* (Pallas Athene); and the authorized biography *Humphrey Jennings* (Picador). He collaborated with the cartoonist Hunt Emerson on several projects, including *Bloke's Progress* (Ruskin Comics), a comic fable inspired by the writings of John Ruskin; a version of Dante's *Inferno* (Knockabout); and, most recently, *Lives of the Great Occultists* (Knockabout). His long narrative poem, *Greta and the Labrador* (Holland House Books) was charmingly illustrated by the artist Jo Dalton. Jackson's other regular collaborators included the cameraman Spike Geilinger, who shot most of his independent films, and the musician Colin Minchin, with whom he co-wrote the rock opera *Bite*. He was a Fellow of the Royal Society of Arts, a Companion of the Guild of St George, and a Regent of the Collège de 'Pataphysique. At his untimely death, Kevin Jackson had completed four of the titles in his Seven Ships Maritime History series. We hope to publish Captain Cook's *Endeavour* in due course. Though each volume tells an independent tale, the series also charts the rise and decline of Britain as the world's greatest naval power.

TSB | Can of Worms will proudly publish Kevin Jackson's wonderful homage to TE Lawrence: *Legion: Thirteen Ways of Looking at Lawrence of Arabia* in 2022. Many moving obituaries were published shortly after Kevin Jackson's death, and links can be found at: www.canofworms.net/KevinJackson.

Production and Publishing Credits

A considerable number of people are involved in realizing an author's work as a finished book on the shelf of your local library, bookshop or online retailer. TSB would like to acknowledge the critical input of:

Cover design, layout and cartography. TSB/Can of Worms has benefited from a longstanding relationship with James Shannon on book production and website development for many of its own titles as well as some of Can of Worms's consultancy clients. For this *Seven Ships Maritime History* Series, James has undertaken the cover design, page layout as well as map design. James and further examples of his work can be found at: www.jshannon.com

Editorial. Editorial has been provided by Tobias Steed, publisher of TSB/Can of Worms. Tobias's career in publishing has spanned forty plus years having started as an editorial assistant for Johns Hopkins University Press in Baltimore, co-founder of illustrated travel guides publishing company, Compass American Guides, Oakland, California, Associate Publisher and Director of New Media at Fodor's/Random House, New York, and most recently founder and publisher of Can of Worms Enterprises Ltd. www.canofworms.net

Ship Plans. Permission for the use of the ship plans in the *Seven Ships Maritime History* series* have been provided to TSB/Can of Worms by Vadiim Eidlin at Best Ship Models, a company that provides accurate ship plans designed especially for model shipbuilders. Their collection includes 500+ plans for beginners and professional modelers. www.bestshipmodels.com

*the plans used in *Darwin's Odyssey: The Voyage of the Beagle* are from Alamy.com

Sales and Marketing. Sales and Marketing. Sales and Marketing for the Seven Ships Maritime History and all other Leapfrog Press titles is overseen by Consortium Book Sales and Distribution (CBSD) St. Paul, Minnesota 55114 www.cbsd.com

Publicity. All publicity enquiries should be directed to Mary Bisbee-Beek. leapfrog@leapfrogpress.com. Further information and resources for the Seven Ships Maritime History series can be found at www.leapfrogpress.com

Seven Ships Maritime History Series – a Note from the author

In the summer of 2006, about five years before the Syrian Civil War began, I spent a couple of weeks in Damascus. In theory I was doing some informal research about Lawrence of Arabia, but in reality I mostly wandered the streets and gazed at the buildings and was touched by the exquisite good manners of the local people. In the afternoons, when the heat became oppressive for a pale European, I went into the Umayyad Mosque – infidels are quite welcome there – and squatted next to one of the pillars, and read the book I had brought with me: a hardback edition of Livingstone Lowes' *The Road to Xanadu,* which is a wonderful exploration of all the travel narratives that fed the imagination of the young Coleridge. It was delicious to escape from the uncomfortable warmth of a Damascene summer and daydream about the snow and the icebergs and the dark, chill waters that the ancient mariners had met when they ventured to the far north.

The extracts from old diaries and letters and memoirs cited in this study re-awoke in me that sense of wonder which the best sailors' tales have always inspired, especially in children. When I put the book down to daydream, I began to think of how fascinating it would be for me to find out more about maritime history, and to tell the stories of the greatest British ships over the centuries of the Western maritime expansion. It was not hard to choose seven famous vessels for seven books, each of which would have its own major themes: *Golden Hind* (exploration, plunder), *Mayflower* (religion, emigration), *Endeavour* (science, colonialism), *Bounty* (rebellion, survival), *Victory* (war, heroism), *Beagle* (biology, genius) and *Endurance* (leadership, heroism, survival). Each volume would be self-contained, but would also mark a chapter in the rise and decline of British maritime power and the creation of the modern world.

The idea came to me whole, in a single dreamy afternoon, and I knew it was what I wanted to do next. Now all I had to do was write my tales: the stories of Seven Ships.

Kevin Jackson, 2020

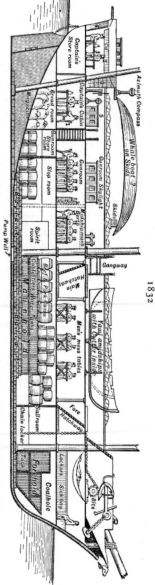

H.M.S. BEAGLE

MIDDLE SECTION FORE AND AFT

1832

1. *Mr. Darwin's Seat in Captain's Cabin*
2. *Mr. Darwin's Seat in Poop Cabin with Cot slung behind him*
3. *Mr. Darwin's Chest of Drawers*
4. *Bookcase*
5. *Captain's Skylight*

Table of Contents

Prologue: The Calm after the Storms

C harles Darwin had endured thirty years of constant hard and often agonisingly dull work. He had been dogged by chronic illness – blinding headaches, agonising stomach cramps, eczema, palpitations, giddiness, and a daily, sometimes hourly, compulsion to vomit. Sometimes these pains were exacerbated by bouts of severe depression that rendered him all but incapable of movement or speech. Melancholy was something that ran in his family, but Charles suffered it more than most of the Darwins, not least in the unbearable months after his most beloved daughter, Annie, died at the age of ten. In middle life he had grown ever more timid, and at times somewhat reclusive. Almost morbidly afraid of offending anyone, and aware that when his alarming theories about the mutability of species were made public many people would be outraged, he had delayed making his conclusions know for twenty years. Another reason for his delay was caution and self-doubt: he wanted to be entirely certain that each of the points he wished to make could be supported by a body of evidence so massive as to be overwhelming. This process had included eight full years engrossed in a minute study of thousands and thousands of barnacles. A distant branch of our family tree.

Gradually, though, at around the start of the 1870s and until his final days, Charles's mood began to lighten. Other, more pugnacious men like his close friend Thomas Huxley had fought the good fight on his behalf. A large part of the civilized world now knew his name, and though angry voices were still raised against him, he was a hero to the thoughtful classes of every nation. Evolution, once an insult to humanity, was now not merely tolerated but enthusiastically embraced by some of the most powerful men and women in the world. Honors poured in from Europe and America, and he was elected to more than sixty learned societies. He was prosperous, powerful, and quietly proud of his accomplishments.

Moreover, as Charles's anxieties decreased, his health improved – strong evidence that the symptoms which had made his life a purgatory for three decades must have been nervous rather than organic in origin. He had always doted on his wife Emma and his children, when breaks from his almost unrelenting labors gave him time for domestic affection. Now he could enjoy their company more frequently and with less divided attention. In later years, they would recall his sweet, gentle nature with fondness. The shy, self-tormenting invalid had become a Victorian patriarch and benevolent squire. And he had changed mankind's view of the world more profoundly than any scientist since Copernicus. More profoundly, perhaps, than any scientist before or since – because the battles for and against his dangerous discovery involved hot emotion as well as cool intellect.

None of this would have happened had he turned down an offer that came to him when he was a hearty, healthy, apparently lazy young man of twenty-two summers.

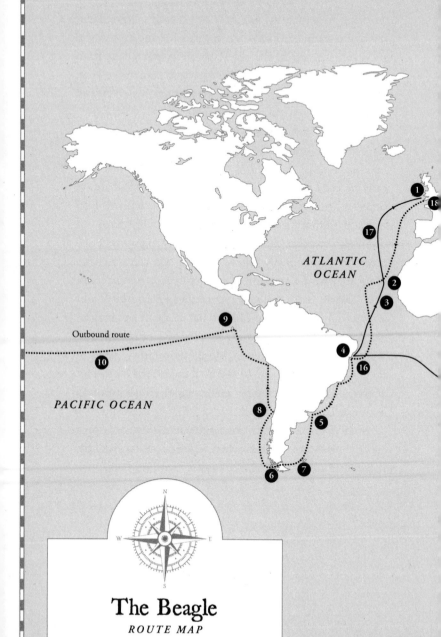

ATLANTIC
OCEAN

PACIFIC OCEAN

Outbound route

The Beagle
ROUTE MAP

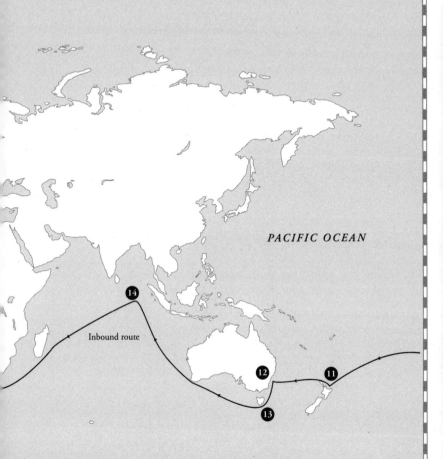

PACIFIC OCEAN

Inbound route

1. Plymouth, England 27 December 1831
2. Cape Verde Islands 16 January 1832
3. St Peter and St Paul Rocks
   15 February 1832
4. Bahia, Brazil 29 February 1832
5. Montevideo, Brazil 29 February 1832
6. Tierra del Fuego 2 December 1832
7. Falkland Islands 10 March 1833
8. Valparaiso, Chile 23 July 1834
9. Galapagos Islands 15 September 1835

10. Tahiti 15 November 1835
11. Bay of Islands, New Zealand
    21 December 1835
12. Sydney, Australia 28 December 1835
13. Hobart, Tasmania 5 February 1836
14. Keeling Island 1 May 1836
15. Cape of Good Hope 31 May 1836
16. Bahia, Brazil 1 August 1836
17. Azores 20 September 1836
18. Falmouth, England 2 October 1836

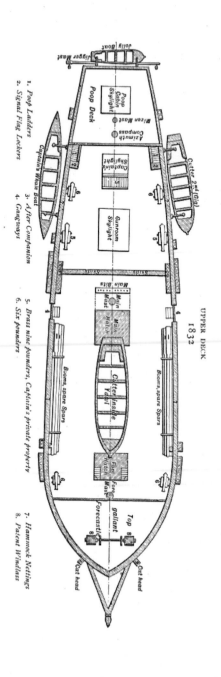

UPPER DECK
1832

1. Poop Ladders
2. Signal Flag Lockers
3. After Companion
4. Gangways
5. Brass nine pounders, Captain's private property
6. Six pounders
7. Hammock Nettings
8. Patent Windlass

Jigger Mast
Jolly Boat
Poop Cabin Skylight
Poop Deck
Mizen Mast
Azimuth Compass
Captain's Whale Boat
Captain's Skylight
Gunroom Skylight
Cutter 2nd (Gig)
STAIR
STAIR
Main Bitts
Main Mast
Main Hatch
Cutter Inside Yawl
Booms, spare Spars
Booms, spare Spars
Fore Hatch
Fore Mast
Fore-gallant
Forecastle
Top
Cat head
Cat head

Chapter 1

Charles the Idler

D r Robert Darwin was angry with his youngest son, Charles. It was the summer of 1831, and the youngest of the Darwin boys looked as if her was wasting his life. "You care for nothing but shooting, dogs and rat-catching, and you will be a disgrace to yourself and all your family", the Doctor shouted at Charles. Many years later, looking back on this outburst, Charles had to agree that his father had not been exaggerating: "He was very properly vehement against my turning [into] an idle sporting man, which then seemed my probable destination ..."

As far as Dr Darwin could see, his son was a three-time failure, who had daydreamed his way through school, dropped out of a medical course in Edinburgh and then spent most of his time at Cambridge riding and hunting by day and drinking and gambling at night. He was not, perhaps, downright stupid, but neither was he all that clever. Charles recalled years later in his *Autobiography*: "I believe I was considered by all my masters and by my

Father as a very ordinary boy, rather below the common standard in intellect."

More dismaying than his sub-average mental ability was Charles's refusal to settle down to pursue a gentlemanly profession. Guessing that neither the Army nor the Law would suit Charles, Dr Darwin lit on the final alternative for the sons of the prosperous: he wanted him to become a clergyman. Charles made only mild objections to this plan, but he was making no effort to study the works of theology that he would need to master. In the summer months following his graduation from Cambridge in 1831 he had done little else but loll around the family house or venture out to destroy large quantities of rural wildlife with his gun.

In many respects, Dr Darwin was quite right. Charles had indeed idled at his formal studies, he had not shown many signs of mental acuity, and he was not burning with ambition to become a parson. But what his father had not noticed was how passionately Charles had been pursuing his "hobbies" – entomology, botany, geology and other aspects of natural history. At most, Dr Darwin thought that the undemanding life of a parson would give his son plenty of leisure time to enjoy such pursuits; indeed, some of England's leading naturalists were clergymen. Many of the country's scientists were still, as they had been for generations, gentleman (and occasionally lady) amateurs – wealthy in their own right, or blessed with virtual sine-cures. It would have astonished him to learn that his son would become respected around the world as the great-est naturalist of his century, or of all time. Fortunately, he lived long enough to take pride in some of his son's astounding accomplishments.

By a quirk of history, Charles Darwin was born on the

same day as another giant figure of the nineteenth century, Abraham Lincoln: 12 February 1809. Charles's grandfather, Erasmus Darwin (1731–1802), had been a famous man of his day, not only as a highly successful medical doctor but also as a "natural philosopher" – the word "scientist" had not yet been coined – and a poet, who used verse as the medium for advancing his various theories. Erasmus, a humane and agreeable man, had propounded a theory of evolution – in fact, one of the most famous of the theories of evolution that had been in the air during the late eighteenth century.

Erasmus Darwin's third son, Robert Waring Darwin (1766–1848), dutifully followed the course set out for him by his father and, after medical studies in Edinburgh and Leyden, settled in the provincial town of Shrewsbury, about 160 miles from London, soon established himself as a prosperous physician and shrewd businessman, and went on to become one of the wealthiest men in the county. Some of his success was due to his unusually sensitive bedside manner. He discovered that quite a few of his patients would get better if he simply sat quietly and listened to them – an antecedent of later types of "talking cure".

Robert Darwin built The Mount, a large house near the river, and in 1796 married Susannah Wedgwood, the oldest daughter of Josiah Wedgwood. The Wedgwood family had grown rich and world famous from their pottery manufacturing business, and there had long been social close ties between the two families, who were also related. They shared Whig politics, supported reforming causes and were ardent voices in the battle against the slave trade. Charles maintained these political allegiances throughout his life.

As a young boy, Charles was doted on by his two older

sisters, who grew ever more protective and possessive of him after his mother died in June 1817, when he was eight years old. Some biographers have speculated that this early experience of loss was at the root of the many illnesses that afflicted him from his thirties onwards; but others have argued that he was given more than enough affection to see him through his bereavement, and that while it is probable that his torments were psychosomatic, their cause needs to be sought elsewhere – perhaps in his early guilt at disappointing a father who had made high demands of him.

In the year his mother died, Charles began to attend a day school nearby, and in 1818 went on to Dr Butler's School in Shrewsbury, where he remained until he was sixteen. The curriculum at Dr Butler's establishment, like that of most British schools of the day, was almost exclusively classical: hours and hours of Latin and Greek, leavened only slightly by ancient Geography and History. Charles, already a keen amateur naturalist, was bored to distraction and, as noted, did not shine in the class-room. Outside the school walls he was a different boy: he would fish, collect shells and other specimens, and go on long solitary walks, fantasizing about the exotic islands and forests he had read about in children's books such as *Wonders of the World*. He and his older brother Erasmus, usually called "Eras", also set up their own laboratory in the garden shed. When Charles's schoolmates heard about the noxious fumes that the brothers were creating, they gave him the nickname "Gas". When he was fifteen Charles was given his first gun, and he discovered that he loved shooting at birds so much that he would actually tremble with excitement. Within a year or so, his love began to border on the obsessive: "How I did enjoy shooting … If there is bliss on earth, that is it … My zeal was so great that I used to place my shooting-boots open by my bed-side when I went to bed, so as not to lose half-a-minute in putting them on in the morning."

Dr Darwin had resolved that his two sons should continue the family tradition and become medical practitioners, so when Charles was sixteen he was sent to Edinburgh to join his brother at the University. Erasmus eventually qualified as a doctor, but never practiced, instead living comfortably on an allowance from their father and cutting an elegant figure as a bachelor in the more fashionable districts of London. Charles never completed his studies, partly because he found many of the lectures tedious, but also because he found the dissection of corpses distressing, and the sight of operations – carried out without the blessing of anesthetics, with the screams of patients rending the air – simply terrifying. When he saw a child being operated on in this brutal, bloody fashion, he ran out of the operating theatre and vowed never to return.

Getting wind of this slackening of attention, Dr Darwin suspected that Charles was losing his way again, and was furious: "If you continue your present indulgent way, your course of study will be utterly useless." Again, it was fair comment, at least as far as medical training was concerned. In reality, though, the teenage Darwin was educating himself very well in other areas. He spent hours wandering along the nearby coast with his brother, collecting marine specimens. He and Eras both read deeply and widely in many subjects, above all in Natural History. He also acquitted himself of an invaluable practical skill: "I am going to learn to stuff birds, from a blackamoor."

Today we find this epithet offensive, but, far from being

disdainful of his new teacher, a former slave by the name of John Edmonstone, Charles reported that he found the older man charming company and highly intelligent. It confirmed the slogan that appeared on a famous image used by the abolitionist movement that he had known from his earliest days: it showed a slave kneeling in chains, and asking "Am I not a man and a brother?" When later in life he met people of other races during his trip around the globe, Darwin took it for granted that they were likely to be as intelligent as any English person, and was happy to concede that some other peoples, such as the Tahitians, were healthier, happier and more beautiful than most white people. Charles also loved hearing about Edmonstone's experiences of tropical countries, which revived his boyhood dreams of travel to hot lands.

Charles passed his second and what was to be his final year in Edinburgh alone, since Eras was pursuing further studies in London. He found the place lonely without his brother, so threw himself into an assortment of extra-curricular activities: he joined various societies, notably the Plinian which hosted talks about science, radical politics and religion. He also found the first important mentor of his life in Dr Robert Grant, a former medical practitioner who had turned his powerful intellect to marine biology, and was a loud and brilliant proponent of evolutionary theory. Darwin had already learned about evolution from his grandfather's writings, but Grant introduced him to the full blast of the revolutionary theories coming out of France, particularly those of Lamarck and St Hilaire. Charles went on long walks with Grant, came to know him well, and caught his intellectual fervor for sea-slugs and sponges.

Grant was pursing an intensive study of marine invertebrates which would very soon establish him as one of the leading scientists in the field. Darwin followed in his footsteps, literally as well as figuratively, and with Grant to guide him began his own marine researches. By the early months of 1827, he was beginning to make small but not insignificant discoveries of his own. Darwin also began to take an interest in geology, and sat in on lectures given by the famous geologist Robert Jameson, which he found fascinating despite the dreariness of their delivery. By the end of his time in Edinburgh, he had learned how to dissect animals, stuff and mount them, and use a microscope. He was entranced by the sights it revealed.

But he had not learned much medicine. In the early summer of 1827 he set off on travels around the country and made his first and last visit to Europe – a short trip to Paris, reluctantly funded by his father. Upon returning to The Mount, Charles threw himself into hunting and socializing. He particularly enjoyed visiting Woodhouse, the country estate of Mr William Mostyn Owen, which was just a short ride away from Shrewsbury. Mr Owen liked Charles, and took the young man with him on long country rambles during which they would shoot hares and birds, talk liberal politics and gossip about family and friends. Compared to the quiet gloom of The Mount, Woodhouse was a place of delicious chaos, large and noisy dinners and hearty drinking. It also offered an additional attraction: Owen's pretty young daughters. Charles's eye was particularly caught by Fanny Owen, a year his senior. Mr Owen was pleased by Charles's obvious interest in Fanny: he had four daughters to marry off soon, and Charles was a fine fellow – excellent son-in-law material.

Fanny was a charming girl, and certainly not a shy one. She flirted, loved attending dances and was almost exhaustingly cheerful. Soon, Charles was entirely smitten; it is hard to tell how she felt about him. They began a correspondence in which her imaginative flights, word-play and teasing seem to teeter on the edge of *double entendre*, but they may have been entirely innocent of serious flirtation. Many years later, one of Charles's sons saw the blissful expression on his father's face as he reminisced about seeing Fanny handle a gun like a true sportsman, and concluded that this must have been the exact moment when Darwin realized he was in love. Love meant marriage, though; and to be married, a young man really ought to have a profession.

Since Robert Darwin had abandoned his well-inten-tioned efforts to coax his son back into medicine, he urged Charles to consider entering the Church or risk finding himself cut off from all financial support. This choice of career may seem almost insane in the light of the damage Darwin's mature work was to inflict on the faithful of many creeds, but Darwin was at this time a believing – if not particularly pious –Anglican and would remain so for years to come. (He was mildly shocked when he first met a man who did not believe in the literal truth of the story of the Flood in Genesis.) Charles hesitated a while, flipped through a few recent books on the Christian faith that quieted the few minor qualms he had about the orthodoxy of his views, and agreed to do what his father said.

At this time, the road to Holy Orders included a degree, so Charles was dispatched to Cambridge, where he matriculated in January 1828 following an intensive period of cramming Greek with a private tutor – for he discovered that he had forgotten absolutely all the Greek he had learned at Butler's School. There was not a free room for him in his college, Christ's, so he lodged for his first terms in a small apartment above a nearby tobacconist's shop. His Cambridge studies would not tax him unduly; he read just enough to scrape by, and otherwise did as he pleased – making new friends, learning to drink (this was the only period of his life when he was in the habit of hearty drinking) and indulging in long reveries about Fanny.

He also discovered a new and to him wholly absorbing pastime: beetles. Throughout his undergraduate days, Darwin's chief pleasure was to head off into the nearby countryside and hunt for specimens, which he also learned to mount. Within two years, he was skilled and learned enough to be able to hold his own in the company of Britain's most eminent entomologists, and he was named in a scholarly journal as the finder of an unknown species. This gave him, he said, the same kind of thrill a poet feels when he sees his first verses in print.

Britain was in a state of intense political turmoil during Darwin's Cambridge years, and his university town was not immune. Angered by what they viewed as the tyranny of University discipline, students rioted, much as the students of the 1960s would do in the following century. Though Charles was seldom directly involved, his sympathy lay with the rebels. And if he was not an open rebel, he was something of a truant, often breaking the nightly curfew; a misdemeanor that put him in some risk of "rustication": being expelled either for a term or for good. He was growing increasingly despondent about his romance with Fanny, who now seldom replied to his letters, and for long periods fell into a state of gloom; nothing like as bad as the depressions that tortured him in later life, but enough to make him discontented.

Science rescued him. He became deeply interested in

the lectures on Botany given by Professor John Stevens Henslow (1796–1861), and before long he was eagerly joining Henslow on field trips – on foot, by coach, or on barges drifting down the rivers Granta and Cam, to examine plants and animals and to enjoy Henslow's discourses. The two men became close friends, and Charles often joined Henslow and his family for dinners. Henslow encouraged Charles to revive his former interest in geology by attending a series of lectures given by Professor Sedgwick. He did so, and was almost instantly converted. It delighted him to see how superbly Sedgwick could teach the subject to beginners. He would take parties out on long rides through the countryside, point out details and fire their imaginations rather than cramming them with facts. Geology, botany and entomology were now the intellectual loves of Charles's life.

Towards the end of his undergraduate days, Charles discovered a book which excited him more than anything he had ever read: Alexander von Humboldt's *Personal Narrative* of his five-year journey through the forests of Brazil (1799–1804); he found it so enthralling and so finely written that he began to dream of making his own expedition. To be exact, he set about trying to organize a scientific mission in Tenerife, about which von Humboldt had rhapsodized, accompanied by a few student friends … and financed by indulgent parents. He worked himself up to such a pitch of excitement that he could hardly sit still, and set out doggedly to learn some Spanish. When not studying, he would sit under a palm tree in Cambridge's botanical gardens, daydreaming about the tropics.

On other matters, he had reason enough to be moody and anxious. Mr Owen had broken the news to him that Fanny had become engaged. It was a bad blow, but as long as she remained unmarried he would not abandon hope. In the meantime, there was the small matter of final examinations.

Charles sat his finals in January 1831, after a few weeks of rapid cramming. He came tenth in his class of 178 passes – a most creditable result after three years largely spent chasing beetles. Cambridge's unusual regulations on residence meant that he had to stay on in town until June, indulging in fantasies about adventures in Tenerife. Meanwhile, Henslow had persuaded Professor Sedgwick to take Charles with him on his annual field trip – the next one being to North Wales.

Charles went home for the early summer, and after some difficult talks father and son came to an understanding. Charles agreed that he would return to Cambridge in October 1831 to begin the studies in Divinity that would pave the path towards priesthood; and Robert allowed his son to enjoy the leisurely long vacation without further argument. He also gave him £200 to pay off his Cambridge debts and, implicitly, to help with the finances of the proposed Tenerife expedition.

He spent most of August in Wales with Sedgwick, receiving a crash course in the elements of geological fieldwork by one of the men best qualified to teach the subject. Sedgwick had two principal aims in mind. First he wanted to check on, and where necessary improve, the details of a geological survey that had been made about a decade earlier, and which he suspected had been rendered out of date by the rapid advances that had taken place in the subject during those years. Second – for reasons that were both scientific and religious – he wanted to examine the fossil record of the area, and to disprove, if he could, a recent contention that fossil deposits provided no evidence that life on earth had passed through successive stages from simple to complex forms. Sedgwick, as pious as he was brilliant, believed that the fossil record was God's writing in the rocks. Sedgwick taught Charles several key lessons. He showed the young man how to "read" a landscape – to recognise how certain types of vegetation and other features pointed to specific underlying formations. He showed Charles how to make diagrams of rock sections, how to mark up a map with geological detail, how to measure escarpments, and how to gather fossils and grasp their significance. In a broader sense, he showed Charles the rudiments of how to think like a geologist.

For the rest of his life, Charles was deeply grateful to Sedgwick for this invaluable training. He returned home to The Mount on 29 August, his head still fizzing with all the skills and knowledge that had been crammed into him. Immediately ahead of him was the agreeable prospect of two weeks of shooting with his uncle; then in October he would go back to Cambridge, do just enough work for his future career in the Church, and start planning the Tenerife trip in earnest. In the event, none of this would happen.

There was a letter waiting for him.

Chapter 2

The Great Opportunity

At the exact time Charles was taking part in Sedgwick's modest geological exercise, *HMS Beagle* was undergoing a major refit. A naval brig, assigned by the Admiralty to cartographic and hydrographic services, she had recently returned from a four-year survey of South America. She was in poor shape, and naval engineers were busy re-sheathing her bottom with planks of fir wood and fresh copper plates, readying her for a second voyage back to the same waters. The mission ahead had two aims: to chart in ever greater detail the coasts of Tierra del Fuego, the Falkland Islands and other areas of military and commercial significance for Britain; and to circumnavigate the globe, using a system of specially designed chronometers. This was the first-ever British attempt at such a circumnavigation.

The *Beagle*'s captain was the 26-year-old Robert Fitz-Roy. Four years older than Charles, he was a slight, dark-complexioned man with a stiff, haughty manner; he was also a man of great intellectual gifts, a fine mathematician and a precociously brilliant sailor, with strong interests in all aspects of science, including Natural History. He had asked one of his colleagues at the Admiralty, Captain Beaufort, if "some well-educated and scientific person should be sought for who would willingly share such accommodations as I had to offer, in order to profit by the opportunity of visiting distant countries yet little known".

FitzRoy's motives were far from purely scientific. To be blunt, he feared for his sanity on the long mission ahead. He was painfully aware that the previous Captain of the *Beagle,* Pringle Stokes, had been so tormented by the loneliness and stress of command in distant seas that he had fallen into a savage depression and shot himself dead, leaving FitzRoy to take over. This was a grim enough precedent, but FitzRoy had further reason to be apprehensive about the trials ahead. Though he was respected for his skills, his efficiency and a degree of humanity unusual in the Navy at this time (though Darwin, unused to the harsh ways of the armed forces, was initially shocked by the brutality of the punishments FitzRoy meted out), FitzRoy knew himself to be a moody, angry and melancholic man. Depression ran in his family. His uncle, the 2nd Marquess of Londonderry – better known as Lord Castlereagh, the British Foreign Secretary – had committed suicide at the age of fifty-three. His doctors, correctly diagnosing a dangerous state of depression, had removed all his razors, so he plunged a pen-knife into his jugular vein. (There were rumors that he was being blackmailed.) What FitzRoy needed was not so much a scientist as an official friend – a civilian friend, outside the system of rank, a man of cultivation and, above all, a member of his own social class: a gentleman.

Beaufort agreed that this was an excellent idea, and he wrote to a Professor Peacock in Cambridge; Peacock in turn consulted his friend Professor Henslow. At first, Henslow was tempted to take up the post himself, but his wife was so distressed at the prospect that he began to look elsewhere. So he wrote to Charles:

> I consider you to be the best qualified person I know of who is likely to undertake such a situation – I state this not in the supposition of yr. being a *finished* naturalist, but as amply qualified for collecting, observing & noting, anything worthy to be noted in Natural History.

> Capt. F. wants a man (I understand) more as a companion than a mere collector & would not take any one no matter how good a Naturalist who was not recommended to him likewise as a *gentleman* ... The voyage is to last **2** years ...

> Don't put any modest doubts or fears about your disqualifications for I assure you I think you are the very man they are in search of – so conceive yourself to be tapped on the Shoulder by your Bum-Bailiff and affectionate friend,

> J.S. Henslow

It was a magnificent opportunity, but Dr Darwin would have none of it. Still the dutiful son, Charles agreed not to go. And yet he could not keep himself from discussing the offer with his kindly uncle, Josiah Wedgwood. On 31 August 1831, Wedgwood sent Dr Darwin a letter in which he addressed each of the eight major objections that the father had outlined to his son, and gave reasons to question their value.

The eight reasons, as paraphrased by Charles, were as follows:

1. Disreputable to my character as a Clergyman hereafter
2. A wild scheme
3. That they must have offered to many others before me, the place of Naturalist
4. And from its not being accepted there must be some serious objection to the vessel or expedition
5. That I should never settle down to a steady life hereafter
6. That my accommodation would be most uncomfortable
7. That you consider it as again changing my profession
8. That it would be a useless undertaking

Josiah's responses were cautiously phrased, thoughtful and convincing. He considered the first objection simply wrong, the next four unlikely, the sixth insignificant, the seventh debatable. He ended by admitting, in response to the eighth and final objection, that "The undertaking would be useless as regards his profession [that is, as a clergyman], but looking upon him as a man of enlarged curiosity, it affords him such an opportunity of seeing men and things as happens to very few". Dr Darwin respected Wedgwood as a man of sense, changed his mind on the spot and not only allowed Charles to set off on the mission but agreed to give him a generous allowance for the various expenses he would meet on the way – since Charles would not be employed on the *Beagle* but would have the status of a paying guest. His board alone would cost his father £50 a year, and there would be other expenses. Greatly to his credit, Dr Darwin never again complained about his son's expenditures; and Charles in turn made every effort not to spend excessively.

But first he had to show Captain FitzRoy that he was the right man. He went to London to meet his potential shipmate. Since first hearing about Charles, FitzRoy had begun to get cold feet about the prospect of living at close quarters with a complete stranger, who might well prove unsympathetic. He already knew that their politics were deeply incompatible: FitzRoy was an aristocrat and a Tory. The first meeting between the two men was nervous on both sides. FitzRoy was frank about the fact that the voyage was going to be no pleasure cruise: there would be storms, danger, discomfort and a claustrophobic lack of space. Oddly, it was FitzRoy's very honesty about these hardships that made Charles first admire him: "... there is something most extremely attractive in his manners, & way of coming straight to the point ... I like his manner of proceeding."

FitzRoy was just as taken by Charles's character – easy-going, modest, intelligent without ostentation, socially refined and keen on the mission ahead. Writing that evening to Beaufort, he conceded: "I like what I see and hear of him, much, and I now request that you will apply for him to accompany me as a naturalist ..."

So Charles won his place on the *Beagle* not by his skills as a geologist, biologist or botanist but by his easy-going ways. Even his charm might not have been enough to win him his place on board if FitzRoy had stuck to his theories about phrenology and physiology. FitzRoy, as Darwin recorded, was

> an ardent disciple of [the leading phrenologist] Lavater and was convinced that he could judge a man's character by the outline of his features; and he doubted whether anyone with my nose could possess sufficient energy and determination for the voyage. But I think he was afterwards well satisfied that my nose had spoken falsely.

For all their differences in politics and temperament, they got along very well for all but a few days on the long voyage – a voyage which, it soon became clear, was going to take a great deal longer than the intended two years. The *Beagle* met with all kinds of trials, above all the storms which lashed her as she sailed further and further south and the winds which slowed her progress to a crawl or forced her to take shelter. Charting took much longer than the Admiralty had realized. In an attempt to speed up their operations, FitzRoy dipped into his own pocket and bought an auxiliary ship, a schooner which he named *Adventure*. He assumed that the Admiralty would approve of his initiative and pay him back; when they refused, he was plunged into a deep depression that almost put an end to the voyage.

And even when not depressed, FitzRoy carried out his mission with a degree of perfectionism that many of the crew found perverse. In the very final weeks of the voyage, when everyone on board was craving the sight of England again, he ordered that they should sail back to the coast of Brazil to double-check some readings. The two-year voyage lasted almost five years.

The *Beagle* had another mission, too – one of FitzRoy's own devising. Beneath his stern and incommunicative exterior he was a devout Christian, and on his earlier *Beagle* adventure had brought three natives of Tierra del Fuego back to England, where they had been converted (at least to FitzRoy's satisfaction), taught English and other lessons and shown how to wear clothes. Together with a young missionary, these three Fuegians would be returned to their native land to spread the Gospel at the bottom of the world.

With FitzRoy, Charles went to see his floating home. He was dismayed: to his eyes it looked more like a wreck than a viable ship, and it was tiny, barely more than 90 feet long. Surely a company of 74, plus supplies and equipment, could not squeeze into such a small space? He was even more downcast when he entered the poop deck, which he would have to share as a living space with two other men: just 10 feet by 11, and so shallow that he had to stoop.

He left the *Beagle* under repair, and made farewell visits to family and friends. At home he heard the ambiguous news that Fanny had broken off her engagement – wonderful news for a future marriage, but terrible timing for a man about to go off on a long voyage. He eventually returned to the *Beagle*'s dock on 24 October, expecting to sail in 10 days' time. But there were delays; and then more delays. He took lodgings near the quay, and began to associate with some of the other senior members of the crew – "senior" more in rank than age, for most of the company were in their early twenties or late teens. One of these seniors was the ship's surgeon, Robert McCormick, who was also the *Beagle*'s official naturalist. Darwin considered McCormick an intellectual lightweight – indeed, an "ass". For his part, McCormick became increasingly resentful of Darwin, first because this paying guest was allowed, unlike McCormick, to dine with the captain, and later because FitzRoy indulged all of Darwin's scientific researches but largely ignored the ambitions of his surgeon.

Charles also began to study trigonometry so as to be able to converse sensibly about navigation, and cursed himself for not having worked harder at mathematics when at school. Day by day, as bad weather postponed the date of sail, his spirits dropped lower, and he recorded his gloom in a new diary. He began to dread the claustrophobia of the poop deck. Fanny, now sad herself, had started sending him letters full of lamentation and wishes that they might take up their courtship again.

He fell into his first serious depression – the blight that would return to him in his early thirties and make his middle years so hard to bear. In later years he wrote:

> Those two months at Plymouth were the most miserable which I ever spent, though I exerted myself in various ways. I was out of spirits at the thought of leaving all my family and friends for so long a time, and the weather seemed to me inexpressibly gloomy. I was also troubled with palpitations and pain about the heart, and like many a young ignorant man, especially one with a smattering of medical knowledge, was convinced that I had heart-disease. I did not consult any doctor, and I fully

expected to hear the verdict that I was not fit for the voyage, and I was resolved to go at all hazards.

Chapter 3

Under Sail (1831–2)

10 December 1831: Sailed, but forced back by storms
21 December: Second attempt to sail; forced back again
27 December: beginning of the circumnavigation

The first, failed attempt to sail from England began at 9 o'clock on the morning of 10 December. Cheers went up on the dockside as the *Beagle* raised her anchor and headed out of port. No sooner were they in open waters than Darwin had to rush to the rail and vomit copiously. It was the first experience of the terrible seasickness that would make so much of his life a misery over the next five years. And all to no purpose: the attempted voyage lasted barely 24 hours. That evening, the *Beagle* was battered by giant waves. Darwin stayed in his hammock in total darkness, hearing the shouts of sailors as he puked and puked. FitzRoy rode out the storm until daybreak, then admitted defeat and headed back to shore.

On 21st December, conditions finally seemed fair

enough for another attempt. Unfortunately, the *Beagle* ran aground almost at once, and could only be freed by the mildly comic expedient of having the whole crew run from one side of the deck to the other, again and again, until the ship began to sway and break loose. They then made good time, and Charles turned in for the night fully expecting to be in the Atlantic when he awoke. Instead, they were returning once again. While Darwin slept, Fitz-Roy had given in to the harsh gales and headed the *Beagle* back to Falmouth.

Third time lucky. On 27th December, after some riotously drunk Christmas revelry left everyone with vile hangovers – even Darwin! – or missing ashore. (The original plan had been to sail on Boxing Day, but no one was in a fit state.) They weighed anchor at 11 o'clock and headed out to sea, and this time there was no need to turn back.

After ten days at sea, horrible seasickness had left Darwin exhausted, undernourished (only a few crumbs of dry biscuit would stay down) and profoundly depressed. Three weeks into the journey, he confided in his diary:

> I often said before starting, that I had
> no doubt I should frequently repent of
> the whole undertaking, little did I think
> with what fervour I should do so. – I can
> scarcely conceive any more miserable state,
> than when such dark and gloomy thoughts
> are haunting the mind as have to-day
> pursued me.

Like many a mariner – Lord Nelson is the most famous suffering sailor – Charles never grew to tolerate seasickness. Almost five years later, towards the end of the epic journey, he wrote:

> I loathe, I abhor the sea and all ships which
> sail on it. Not even the thrill of geology
> makes up for the misery and vexation of
> spirit that comes with sea-sickness.

There were other miseries to dampen his spirits. His first witnessing of the Royal Navy's iron code of disciple appalled him – FitzRoy had the most hooligan of the Christmas revelers flogged, and the sound of their anguished screams was dreadful. (To his surprise, the crew did not seem to bear any grudges.) Then came a major disappointment: the plan had been that the *Beagle* would stop for some welcome shore leave at Tenerife – the very place Charles had dreamed of exploring whilst at Cambridge. The *Beagle* came in to dock on 6th January, only to be intercepted by a small boat carrying orders that she was to be put in quarantine for 12 days, for fear that she might be importing cholera to the island.

FitzRoy, decisive as ever, immediately ordered the ship under full sail, and headed back out to sea. The move crushed Darwin's hopes of exploration so completely that he spoke of the quarantine orders as a "death warrant". But at least he was over the worst of his initial seasickness, and was just about well enough to read the first volume of Lyell's *Principles of Geology* – the book that was to influence him more than any other during his odyssey. And, having got over his shock at the Captain's merciless enforcement of naval discipline, he was beginning to get on well with FitzRoy, who had taken minutes away from his pressing duties during their first abortive sail to make the suffering Darwin a little more comfortable in his hammock.

The two men were delighted to discover that they shared a fondness for the novels of Jane Austen.

Charles didn't have much longer to wait until he could see tropical landscapes at close range.

16 January 1832: First view of tropics

His first view of the tropics was the sight of St Jago, one of the Cape Verde Islands, about 450 miles off the coast of West Africa. The *Beagle* anchored there on 16th January 1832, having sighted the Peak of Tenerife, veiled in its lower parts by clouds, the previous day: "This was the first of many delightful days never to be forgotten." Setting the pattern to which he would adhere for the rest of the voyage, Darwin began to explore as soon as he could, and found that Von Humboldt's magical descriptions of exotic forests were no more than a pale evocation of the true splendors of the tropics. He was in "a perfect *hurricane* of delight and astonishment" – and his joy only deepened as he made new discoveries: kingfishers, sponges and corals, wild cats and marine life:

> I was much interested, on several occasions, by watching the habits of an Octopus, or cuttle-fish ... They darted tail first, with the rapidity of an arrow, from one side of the pool to the other, at the same instant discolouring the water with a dark chestnut-brown ink. These animals also escape detection by a very extraordinary, chameleon-like power of changing their colour ...

Inspired by Lyell's *Principles*, he also began to ask himself questions about the geology of the island. In the rocks, about thirty feet above sea level, he discovered a vein of white matter which proved to be compressed shells and coral. Darwin was still something of a beginner in the earth sciences, but it was plain enough to him that this vein indicated that the place had once been under water. Yet Lyell's pages had told him that the earth changes only very, very slowly … He pondered the matter, and came to the interim conclusion that, since there was no sign of cataclysmic activity in the white strip, Lyell's gradualism was almost certainly the right explanation. He worked excitedly and intensely, until it was time – on 8th February – to return to sea and the horrors of seasickness.

Chapter 4

In South America

15 February 1832: Landed at St Paul's Rocks
29 February 1832: Landed at Bahia, Brazil

On 15th February 1832, the *Beagle* put into the St Paul Islands, some 549 miles from the South American coast, and the crew went on a frenzy of gull-killing and egg-hunting, to replenish their food stocks. The following day they crossed the Equator, and celebrated the achievement with the Navy's traditional "Crossing the Line" pranks. FitzRoy cast off his usual austerity and dressed up as Father Neptune. Each of the equatorial virgins – thirty-two in all – was called to the forecastle where half-naked sailors scampered and pranced, their bodies daubed in bright paints. Darwin was the first victim; genuinely alarmed at the wild behavior of the sailors, he ran for it. But they grabbed him, blindfolded him and tossed him into an outstretched sail that had been filled with water. After dragging him out,

They then lathered my face & mouth with
pitch and paint, & scraped some of it off with
a piece of roughened iron hoop. – a signal
being given I was tilted head over heels into
the water, where two men received me &
ducked me. – at last, glad enough, I escaped
... The whole ship was a shower bath: &
water was flying about in every direction: of
course not one person, even the Captain, got
clear of being wet through.

But there was no animosity behind this rough-housing.
The crew had all come to like Charles, and, following
FitzRoy's example, had begun to address him using the
affectionate nickname "Philos" – short for "Philosopher".

Throughout his mature life, people would comment
on Charles's appealing modesty, and his ability to get on
with men, women and children of all descriptions. One
writer who met him when he was old and famous actually remarked that he showed a degree of humility that
bordered on the "pathetic" in such an eminent man. Nineteenth-century Britain was a society in which members of
different classes seldom met as equals, yet Darwin never
found it difficult to make friends with those who were not
"gentlemen" like himself. He would happily chat for hours
with horse-grooms, pigeon-fanciers, gardeners, ditch-dig-
gers and farmers, politely tapping each one for his particular expertise. Some of his easiness of manner was due to
his having been forced into close contact with the crew of
the *Beagle*, after a sheltered early life spent mostly among
the landed gentry and the wealthy. Though he initially
found the sailors dismayingly loud and coarse, he soon
came to admire them for their stoicism and resourceful-

ness. They, in turn, warmed to his willingness to muck in and his cheerful demeanor. In this sense, Darwin was an instinctive egalitarian. His sense of human potential – and its failures – was extended still further by the people he met ashore, from rich estate owners and earnest missionaries to the beautiful Tahitians and the far from comely Fuegians. In later years, he would think deeply about the nature of societies, and how they might be seen to have evolved just like other living things. If the *Beagle* voyage was the making of him as a naturalist, it also taught him the basics of another science, one that did not fully mature until the twentieth century: anthropology.

The *Beagle* sailed on into increasingly hot climes; Charles was too warm to sleep properly in his cabin, so he would often go up on deck at night to watch the Southern Cross and other constellations. Eventually, on 28th February, they made landfall on the coast of Brazil, at the port of Bahia, later renamed Salvador. For the next six months, the *Beagle* sailed the coasts of Brazil and Uruguay, from Bahia southwards to the Rio de la Plata – about 2,000 miles in all. On 29th February, Charles set out on his first venture into a Brazilian forest. It was a rapturous experience. That night, he wrote in his diary:

> The day has passed delightfully. Delight
> itself, however, is a weak term to express
> the feelings of a naturalist who, for the first
> time has wandered by himself in a Brazilian
> forest. The elegance of the grasses, the
> novelty of the parasitical plants, the beauty
> of the flowers, the glossy green of the
> foliage, but above all the general luxuriance
> of the vegetation, filled me with admiration.

(The word "admiration" has weakened somewhat since Darwin's day, when it was closer to its original meaning of "wonder" or "awe".)

This magnificent vision was almost snatched away from Darwin, when he had a bitter argument with FitzRoy that might easily have caused the angry Captain to have him sent home. The issue was slavery. Darwin had been noticing how the local economy was based on the forced labor of slaves. As the offspring of two Whig parents who had both been passionately committed to the emancipation movement, Darwin was disgusted and outraged. But FitzRoy had very different views. Darwin recalled in his *Autobiography* that:

> ... early in the voyage at Bahia in Brazil he defended and praised slavery, which I abominated, and told me that he had just visited a great slave-owner, who had called up many of his slaves and asked them whether they were happy, and whether they wished to be free, and all answered "No." I then asked him, perhaps with a sneer, whether he thought that the answers of slaves in the presence of their master was worth anything. This made him excessively angry, and he said that as I doubted his word, we would not live any longer together.

To FitzRoy's credit, his rage was short-lived:

> I thought that I should have been compelled to leave the ship; but as soon as the news

spread, which it did quickly, as the captain sent for the first lieutenant to assuage his anger by abusing me, I was deeply gratified by receiving an invitation from all the gun-room officers to mess with them. But after a few hours Fitz-Roy showed his usual magnanimity by sending an officer to me with an apology and a request that I would continue to live with him.

Fortunately, such explosions were rare, for FitzRoy was fond of his civilian guest. He wrote to Beaufort:

Darwin is a very sensible, hard-working man and a very pleasant mess-mate. I never saw a 'shore-going fellow' come into the ways of a ship so soon and so thoroughly as Darwin. I cannot give a stronger proof of his good sense and disposition than by saying 'Everyone respects and likes him' ...

27–28 March: Abrolhos
5 April: Rio de Janeiro

On 18th March, having drawn up a detailed map of the harbor, FitzRoy set sail from Bahia and took soundings along the Abroholos islets, in the direction of Rio de Janeiro. Two weeks later, the crew did not fail to take advantage of April Fool's Day: as the clocks showed midnight, one of them ran into Charles's cabin and shouted, "Darwin, did you ever see a grampus?". Charles raced up on deck, only to be greeted by gales of laughter.

They arrived in Rio de Janeiro on 5th April 1832.

Before the crew had even lowered the sails, a mail bag was thrown on board, with many letters from home for Charles. His sisters' letters were full of gossip, especially about marriages. His sister Charlotte had married an amiable parson; she was keener than ever that Charles should come home to set himself up as a rural clergyman and take a wife. Charles still thought it possible that he might follow his family's wishes and take Holy Orders; Holy Matrimony was another matter. By the same post he learned that his former intended, Fanny Owen, had become engaged to one Robert Biddulph. His immediate reaction was shock. Admirably stoical as he could be in the face of discomfort and danger, he was keenly vulnerable to emotional wounds. He wept and wept, repeating the words "my dearest Fanny".

Partly to put this dreadful dashing of hopes out of his mind, he set out on a grueling trek a hundred miles to the north of Rio with some British residents of the city, to an estate run by an Englishman. The heat made him ill and the riding exhausted him, though sightings of animals and plants en route were a generous recompense. When they reached the estate, Darwin wished they had not come. Once again he was confronted with the moral horrors of slavery, when the estate owner – entirely pleasant and generous to Europeans – showed himself tyrannical to his slaves. After an angry quarrel with his foreman, the Englishman threatened to sell the man's favorite illegitimate child at auction in Rio, and then went on to swear that he would also sell all the other enslaved women and children of the area.

More shocking still was Darwin's own first-hand experience of the terror that white people inspired in black slaves. He was trying to make himself understood to a tall, strapping slave by making hand gestures:

I talked loud, and made signs, in the course
of which I passed my hand near his face.
He, I suppose, thought I was in a passion,
and was going to strike him; for instantly,
with a frightened look and half-shut eyes,
he dropped his hands. I shall never forget
my feelings of disgust, and shame, at seeing
a great powerful man afraid even to ward
off a blow, directed, as he thought, at
his face. This man had been trained to a
degradation lower than the slavery of the
most helpless animal.

After a few days of exploring the nearby jungle, days in which he brooded on his lost love, he came back to Rio to discover that the *Beagle* was about to take off on surveying duties until July. He decided to stay for the duration, and rented a cottage at Botofogo Bay: "It was impossible to wish for anything more delightful than thus to spend some weeks in so magnificent a country." He shared his lodgings with the *Beagle*'s artist, Augustus Earle, whose lively company he enjoyed, and one of the Fuegians, Miss Fuegia Basket.

25 April – 25 June. Darwin lived at Botafogo

Every day, Darwin worked hard, either hunting for specimens or preparing them to be sent home; and he wrote many letters, including a long and detailed scientific one to Henslow. On 23rd June, the *Beagle* returned to Rio. The news was grim: three men had died of fever after a snipe-shooting party. And the crew had also lost a fourth member – but this was not such bad news. Resentful and

envious of what he had come to see as FitzRoy's ostenta-
tiously preferential treatment of Darwin – a mere civilian! – the ship's surgeon and official naturalist, Robert
McCormick, had quit the expedition and gone back to
England. This suited Darwin very well; though he was
never appointed as the *Beagle*'s official naturalist, everyone from now on treated him precisely as though he were.
Still in reality a paying guest, Darwin now felt like a true
member of the Royal Navy.

On 1st July 1832, he and his shipmates attended a
religious service on board another British vessel, the
Warsprite, and Darwin found himself unexpectedly stirred
at the company's cries of "God Save the King!" Four days
later, the *Beagle* sailed out of Rio and southwards towards
Montevideo, meeting heavy seas and chilling weather.
Once again, Darwin suffered badly from seasickness, and
tried to keep his mind from misery by reading one of his
favorite books, John Milton's epic poem *Paradise Lost.*
Nature also provided distractions:

> ... we witnessed a splendid scene of natural
> fireworks; the mast-head and yard-arm-ends
> shone with St Elmo's light; and the form
> of the vane could almost be traced, as if it
> had been rubbed with phosphorous. The sea
> was so highly luminous, that the tracks of
> the penguins were marked by a fiery wake,
> and the darkness of the sky was momentarily
> illuminated by the most vivid lightning.

FitzRoy had intended to return to Buenos Aires for a brief
stay, but was infuriated when a Brazilian gunship fired a
warning shot over the *Beagle*. He loaded the ship's guns

and messaged the guard ship that he would retaliate if a
second shot were fired.

26 July – 19 August: Montevideo

Excitement mounted when the *Beagle* reached Montevideo on 26th July. Almost at once, the local chief of police called on FitzRoy to put down a rebellion: black soldiers had taken over the town's central fort, which was also an arsenal. FitzRoy promptly dispatched 50 armed sailors … and also Darwin, who was thrilled at the chance to see action. He kitted himself out with pistols in his belt and a cutlass in his hand, and felt quite bloodthirsty. FitzRoy thoroughly approved of Darwin's unexpectedly swash-buckling manner:

> Darwin is a regular trump ... He has a
> mixture of necessary qualities which makes
> him feel at home, and happy, and makes
> everyone his friend.

But the rebels had little fight in them, and surrendered almost without effort. A shade disappointed by having missed out on some real fighting, Darwin noted that

> there certainly is a great deal of pleasure in
> the excitement of this sort of work – quite
> sufficient to explain the reckless gayety
> with which sailors undertake even the most
> hazardous attacks.

Charles settled in Maldonado, and for the next ten weeks made ventures into the countryside, collecting animal and bird specimens. He also made an excursion to the Polanko river, accompanied by two heavily armed bodyguards. On the first day out they heard that the body of a traveler, his throat a gory, gaping wound, had been found on their road just the day before.

It was on this trip, in a "*pulepria*" or drinking-shop, that Darwin first met a class of men with whom he would soon become familiar: gauchos.

> During the evening, a great number of
> Gauchos came in to drink spirit and smoke
> cigars: their appearance is very striking;
> they are generally tall and handsome, but
> with a proud and dissolute expression of
> countenance. They frequently wear their
> moustaches and long hair curling down
> their backs. With their brightly coloured
> garments, great spurs clanking about their
> heels, and knives stuck as daggers (and
> often so used) at their waists, they look a
> very different race of men from what might
> be expected from their name of Gauchos,
> or simple countrymen. Their politeness
> is excessive; they never drink their spir-
> its without expecting you to taste it; but
> whilst making their exceedingly graceful
> bow they seem quite as ready, if occasion
> offered, to cut your throat.

Darwin befriended these charismatic fellows, and they taught him some of their skills. Darwin was a good rider and an excellent shot, which impressed them greatly. He was less impressive when he tried his hand at using their famous balls, or "*bolas*":

> One day, as I was amusing myself by
> galloping and whirling the balls round
> my head, by accident the free one struck
> a bush; and its revolving motion being
> thus destroyed, it immediately fell to the
> ground, and, like magic, caught one hind
> leg of my horse; the other ball was then
> jerked out of my hand, and the horse fairly
> secured ... The Gauchos roared with laugh-
> ter; they cried out that they had seen every
> sort of animal caught, but had never before
> seen a man caught by himself.

On 19th August, Darwin sent Henslow his first box of specimens, and later that day the *Beagle* set off on a series of charting missions along the Patagonian coastline. When next they put ashore, it was at a remote, hazardous settlement in dangerous territory: Bahia Blanca.

6 September – 17 October: Bahia Blanca
26–30 October: Montevideo
2–10 November: Buenos Aires

Bahia Blanca was set in the middle of a war zone – the war being waged, with ruthless ferocity on both sides, by the native Indians and the colonizing Spanish. Rumor had it that Englishmen, being neutral, were usually safe enough, provided they carried guns and money for bribes. Darwin had more personal anxieties in mind, though: he had heard that the French government had sponsored a scientist, Alcide d'Orbigny, to undertake a six-year collecting mission. Darwin wrote to Henslow that he was worried that the Frenchman would already have taken "the cream of all the good things".

On the contrary: over the next couple of weeks, Darwin found some of the most exciting specimens of the whole trip. On 22nd September he came across some fossils in excellent condition – the teeth and thigh bone of some extinct creature, almost certainly a mammal. Some days later he discovered a vast skull, and on 8th October found a large jawbone, with a distinctive tooth that confirmed he had come upon the remains of a "megatherium" – a distant relative of the present-day sloth. By the time the *Beagle* sailed again, he had amassed fossil remains of six different species.

On 19th October, the *Beagle* set off on its return journey to Montevideo. Again, Darwin tried to take his mind off the miseries of seasickness by reading Milton. At Montevideo there was a new consignment of mail from England. There was political gossip – the country was undergoing such a radical series of reforms that the Tories feared Revolution – and romantic gossip: his sister Catherine was keen that Charles should come back to England and marry a different Fanny: Miss Fanny Wedgwood. Cholera was still raging in some parts of Great Britain, and was threatening his home town. Darwin wrote to one of his friends that he still dreamed of the easy and tranquil life of a country parson, but "the Captain says if I indulge in such visions, as green fields & nice little wives, &c &c, I shall certainly make a bolt … I must remain contented with sandy plains and great Megatheriums."

It was time to set out on what the devoutly Christian FitzRoy considered one of the most important tasks of their voyage: the return of the three Anglicized Fuegians to their old home. Before heading south, they made a short trip up the River Plate to Buenos Aires, where Darwin loaded up with personal supplies – notebooks, pens, cigars – and saw a dentist. Strolling around town, he was much taken by the elegance and seductiveness of the female half of the population – "angels gliding down the streets…" – and wrote only half-jokingly to his sisters, "It would do the whole tribe of you a great deal of good to come to Buenos Ayres".

14–26 November: Montevideo

Back for a final stay in Montevideo, Darwin worked long and hard to prepare his next shipment of specimens to Henslow. He also found time to read the eagerly awaited second volume of Lyell's *Principles*, which struck Darwin as brilliantly argued. It dealt with the subject of how species become extinct and are created; and it contended that there was no mechanism in nature to help animals modify themselves as their environment changed. At this point, Darwin was still very much impressed by Lyell's style of argument, as well as his profound erudition. He continued to view landscapes through the lenses that Lyell had cut; but the months ahead would give him all the evidence he needed that, however sound Lyell might be on rocks, he was quite wrong about creatures.

Tired out following his recent efforts, Charles was in low spirits, and none too happy with the prospect of what was to come next: Tierra del Fuego, The Land of Fire.

Chapter 5

The Land of Fire

2 December 1832 – 26 February 1833: Tierra del Fuego

On 21st December 1832 the *Beagle* rounded Cape Horn, and the company spent a miserable Christmas sheltering in a small cove. The gales were fierce, and the temperatures plummeted. The crew had foreseen these bitterly chill conditions, and on the journey southwards they had already begun to dress more warmly, and try to toughen themselves up:

> Everyone has put on cloth cloathes, and preparing for still greater extremes, our beards are all sprouting. My face at the present looks of about the same tint as a half-washed chimney sweeper. With my pistols in my belt and geological hammer in hand, shall I not look like a grand barbarian?

It was now that FitzRoy's evangelical zeal, usually concealed from the company beneath his stern mask of command, became fully apparent. Though his main duty was to the Admiralty, he felt that he had a still more pressing duty to his Maker, and he wished to establish Christianity in the far south of the Americas. And so, as well as bringing home his three Fuegian (supposed) converts, he had raised money to finance a young cleric, Richard Matthews, as the first missionary in Tierra del Fuego. Since most supporters of missionary work believed that Christianity and civilized habits were the two sides of the coin of Progress, Matthews was charged not only with preaching the Gospel and teaching English but also with showing the Fuegians how to build houses, farm, wear European-style clothes and wash themselves. Up to this point, even his closest on-board companion, Darwin – himself still a believing Christian, of course – had not been aware of quite how seriously FitzRoy took this unofficial, religious aspect of their voyage.

The first landing party was to include the three Fuegians the captain had captured on the *Beagle*'s previous mission: Fuegia Basket (originally Yokcushlu) – a girl of about thirteen, shy, intelligent and a very gifted linguist; Jemmy Button (Orundellico) – plump, affectionate, smartly dressed and self-important; and York Minster (El'leparu) – a reserved, rather sullen man of about thirty, who clearly understood more English than he would admit. It was assumed by all that Miss Basket and Mr Minster were engaged to be married, though quite what kind of marriage they envisaged was not clear.

In the course of the long journey, Darwin had grown fond of the Fuegians, whom he treated as he would have treated honest, simple English countrymen and women.

This friendship confirmed the impression he had formed while studying in Edinburgh, when he had forged a friendship with John Edmonstone the taxidermist: that all races of the human species were equally intelligent.

> The American aborigines, Negroes and
> Europeans are as different from each
> other in mind as any three races that can
> be named; yet I was incessantly struck,
> whilst living with the Fuegians on board
> the *Beagle*, with the many little traits of
> character, showing how similar their minds
> were to ours; and so it was with a full-
> blooded negro [that is, Mr Edmonstone]
> with whom I happened once to be intimate.

So it came as a genuine shock to Darwin when he caught his first glimpse of local men watching them from land:

> I shall never forget how savage & wild one
> group was. – Four or five men suddenly
> appeared on a cliff near to us, – they were
> absolutely naked & with long streaming
> hair; springing from the ground & waving
> their arms around their heads, they sent
> forth most hideous yells. Their appearance
> was so strange, that it was scarcely like
> that of earthly inhabitants.

It reminded him, he said, not so much of the demons in *Paradise Lost* as of the devils in Weber's lurid supernatural opera *Der Fresischutz*, which he had seen in Edinburgh. It was a little frightening, but it also thrilled him, as did the big fires that blazed on the shores in response to their passage. When FitzRoy took a small party ashore at their first anchorage, Darwin went with him; it was, he said, the "most curious & interesting spectacle I ever beheld". Fitz-Roy reacted stiffly to the locals' hearty overtures of friendship, but Darwin was much less inhibited, and thoroughly enjoyed his attempts at non-verbal communication. At one point he and an elderly Fuegian walked along the beach patting their breasts in unison and making funny noises, as if calling chickens. Darwin was also fascinated to see how the natives responded with incredulity upon seeing Jemmy Button in all his European finery. It was clear that both the visitors and locals were at once amused, disconcerted and baffled by each other.

Soon, the *Beagle*'s own trio were protesting vehemently that the natives were uncouth, unpleasant, shameful creatures; Button angrily called them "monkeys – dirty – fools – not men". They were behaving exactly like a British family who had suddenly come up in the world, and refused to acknowledge their poor relatives. It gave Darwin food for many years of thought:

> I could not have believed how wide was
> the difference, between savage and civilised
> man. It is greater than that between a wild
> and domesticated animal ...

In later years, he pondered on the apparent inability of the Fuegians to rise above their bleak circumstances through the exercise of reason:

> What is there for imagination to picture, for
> reason to compare, for judgment to decide

upon? To knock a limpet from the rock
does not even require cunning, that lowest
power of the mind. Their skill in some
respects may be compared to the instinct of
animals; for it is not improved by experience: the canoe, their most ingenious work,
poor as it is, has remained the same, for the
last two hundred and fifty years.

Had it really taken only a little over three years in England
for their "savage" friends to be so thoroughly transformed
into the polite, agreeable shipmates he liked so well?
Apparently so: a fact which deepened Darwin's conviction that the wicked institution of slavery was based on a
nonsensical biological theory – that humans with darker
skins constituted a different species (a viewpoint that
quite a few European scientists sincerely held and eagerly
promoted). But he also grasped the dark side of this
phenomenon. If civilization could be attained so rapidly,
might it not be stripped away with equal speed?

By the end of January, the ship's company had helped
build the Mission station, in Woollya Sound, where Jemmy
Button used to live. Sadly, Jemmy seemed to have forgotten his native language, and his attempts to talk with his
fellow countryman were futile; nor did he seem keen on
re-establishing affectionate relations with his family. He
showed no sign of grief when told that his father had died;
he merely insisted repeatedly that it had not been his fault.
Darwin was disappointed at the locals' habit of stealing
everything they could not beg, and alarmed when, after a
few days, the atmosphere began to grow hostile. One man
made the unmistakable gestures of carving up a human
body. But things seemed to calm down, and FitzRoy was

reassured enough to leave Matthews on his own for a few weeks while the *Beagle* went back to its surveying duties.

It was a bad decision. Upon their return, Matthews ran screaming towards them, begging to be brought to safety on board. A band of Fuegians had been entertaining themselves by holding him down and pulling the hairs out of his beard one by one, using mussel shells as pincers. He refused to go back on shore. But the three Fuegians of the *Beagle* took quite a different attitude, and – for some reason believing that Jemmy's family and friends were a cut above the natives they had first encountered, and despised – decided to stay. Everyone was sad to say goodbye. In the face of this disappointing outcome, FitzRoy consoled himself by reflecting that, perhaps, even without the help and guidance of an English Man of God, their former shipmates would keep to their civilized ways and gradually improve and enlighten their countrymen.

The *Beagle* set sail for the Falklands on 26th February.

1 March – 6 April: East Falkland Island

The crew came into harbor at Port Louis and were surprised to see the Union Flag flying; as they soon discovered, two British warships – the *Clio* and the *Tyne* – had arrived in January in response to the Argentinean government's assertion of their territorial right to the islands they knew as the Malvinas, and reclaimed the islands for the Crown. Mr Woodbine Parish, the British Chargé d'Affaires in Buenos Aires, had demanded that British sovereignty be restored. This swift act of retaliation and repossession had outraged popular opinion throughout South America, and particularly in Argentina: "I suppose the occupation of this place, has only just been noted in the English paper [*sic*]," Darwin wrote to his sister Caroline, "but we hear all the Southern part of America is in a ferment about. By the aweful language of Buenos Ayres one would suppose this great Republic meant to declare war against England!" Darwin was moved to scorn, and imagined the Argentinean government talking of "a just revolt" and lamenting "their poor subjects groaning under the tyranny of England ..."

FitzRoy and his men carried out a detailed survey while Darwin drudged around in the cold, wet and desolate landscape, breaking rocks, shooting at the odd bird, and trying to capture specimens of the scanty wildlife. He was delighted to discover some sand-stones which, tapped with a hammer, yielded fossil molluscs, similar to the ones he had seen in Wales on his modest explorations with Sedgwick. When he returned to England, he would have the chance to compare fossils culled from locations that were thousands of miles apart. The *Beagle* weighed anchor on 6th April, and set sail for the mainland.

Bad weather forced the *Beagle* away from her intended destination, the mouth of the Rio Negro, and towards Maldonado, some 65 miles east of Montevideo. Having realized that the task of surveying was far slower than either he or the Admiralty had anticipated, FitzRoy decided that the best policy would be to dip into his own pockets and buy a second ship, a schooner owned by a seal-hunter, which could make independent surveys. In the long term this would speed up their task considerably, but in the short term it meant several months of delay: the new schooner would have to be fitted out with a copper bottom.

28 April – 3 July: Living in Maldonado

During the refitting, Darwin took lodgings in Maldonado and used the town as a base for expeditions. His main trip began on 9th May, when he set off for a two-week jaunt with a pair of guides. He was in high spirits at being back on the mainland, and he collected hundreds of specimens, recruiting small boys by offering them coins in return for dead mammals and snakes; bird species he mostly slaughtered himself.

The messy, smelly and tedious job of dissecting, skinning, and otherwise investigating these mounds of dead flesh and noxious juices soon become too much for Charles to do on his own, so he took on the services of the *Beagle*'s sixteen-year-old cabin boy, Syms Covington, who soon became highly competent in the skills Darwin taught him. He was so pleased with Syms that he offered to take him off FitzRoy's accounts and pay for his labors from his own pocket. FitzRoy approved, and let Darwin employ the lad at the bargain rate of just thirty pounds a year. He would remain in Darwin's service until 1839.

On 24th July, the *Beagle* and the now-shipshape schooner, named *Adventure,* sailed south for the Rio Negro.

3–11 August: Rio Negro

The *Beagle* arrived at the mouth of the Rio Negro in Argentina on 3rd August. As they sailed along, Darwin noted the ruins of several "*estancias*" which had been destroyed a few years earlier by the Indians: "Araucanians from the south of Chile; several hundreds in number, and highly disciplined." They stopped at a small settlement built on the riverbank: "The town is indifferently called El Carmen or Patagones." Here, they encountered Indians who were "considered civilized" by the local government. Some of them had recently been employed on a sealing mission, where they had performed well:

> They were now enjoying the fruits of their labour, by being dressed in very gay, clean clothes, and by being very idle. The taste they showed in their dress was admirable; if you could have turned one of these young Indians into a statue of bronze, his drapery would have been perfectly graceful.

11 August – 8 September: Overland trip from Rio Negro to Bahia Blanca

Darwin set off on a long expedition from Patagones to Bahia Blanca. "Mr. Harris, an Englishman residing at Patagones, a guide, and five Gauchos who were proceeding on to the army on business, were my companions on the journey." On the way, they encountered several sights that Darwin found fascinating, including a locally famous tree that "the Indians reverence as the altar of [their god] Walleechu" – or perhaps as the god himself. He began to take increasingly keen pleasure in the journey, especially when they stopped to camp on the shores of the Rio Colorado:

> This was the first night which I passed under the open sky, with the gear of the recardo for my bed. There is high enjoyment in the independence of the Gaucho life – to be able at any moment to pull up your horse, and say: "Here we will

pass the night." The death-like stillness
of the plain, the dogs keeping watch, the
gipsy-group of gauchos making their beds
around the fire, has left in my mind a
strongly marked picture of this night which
will not soon be forgotten.

Close by them was the encampment of General Juan
Manuel de Rosas, who was leading the war against the
Indians. Initially, Darwin was impressed:

General Rosas intimated a wish to see me;
a circumstance which I was afterwards very
glad of. He is a man of an extraordinary
character, and has a most predominant
influence in the country, which it seems he
will use to its prosperity and advancement...

But in a later edition of *Voyage of the Beagle*, published in
1845, Darwin added the glum footnote: "This prophecy
has turned out entirely and miserably wrong." For one
thing, as he soon realized, Rosas was conducting what
was in effect a war of extermination: a genocide of all the
Indians who would not come under his command. For
another, Rosas set himself up as a dictator.

Darwin's company rode on towards Bahia Blanca, stop-
ping on the way at a post-house which once again led him
to ponder the essential equality of the races:

This posta was commanded by a negro
lieutenant, born in Africa: to his credit let
it be said, there was not a ranche between
the Colorado and Buenos Ayres in nearly

such neat order as his ...

I did not anywhere meet a more civil
and obliging man than this negro; it was
therefore the more painful to see that he
would not sit down and eat with us.

Chapter 6

El Naturalista Don Carlos

"**B**ahia Blanca scarcely deserves the name of a village," Darwin wrote, being barely more than a barracks and a few houses. He asked the Commandant to lend him a guide and some fresh horses, and rode out towards the harbor to see whether the *Beagle* had yet arrived. Though the countryside was largely wasteland, it was abundant in ostriches, deer and armadillos – one of which he killed, roasted and ate with his companion. It was not enough food for a single day, but Darwin was more troubled by thirst than hunger:

> Our horses were very poor ones, and in
> the morning they were soon exhausted
> from not having had anything to drink, so
> that we were obliged to walk. About noon
> the dogs killed a kid, which we roasted. I
> ate some of it, but it made me intolerably
> thirsty. This was the more distressing as

the road, from some recent rain, was full
of little puddles of clear water, yet not a
drop was drinkable. I had scarcely been
twenty hours without water, and only
part of the time under a hot sun, yet the
thirst rendered me very weak. How people
survive two or three days under such
circumstances, I cannot imagine: at the
same time, I must confess that my guide
did not suffer at all, and was astonished
that one day's deprivation should be so
troublesome to me.

Darwin's stay in Bahia Blanca came at a time of intense
agitation and rumors of the war between Rosas' troops
and the Indians. One day, the town received reports that
Indians had attacked and killed several men, stationed at
one of the *postas* on the route to Buenos Aires. The next
day, three hundred troops arrived, many of them *manso*
(literally "tame") Indians. *Manso* did not seem quite the
right word for their behavior:

They passed the night here; and it was
impossible to conceive anything more wild
and savage than the scene of their bivouac.
Some drank until they were intoxicated;
others swallowed the steaming blood of the
cattle slaughtered for their suppers, and
then, being sick from drunkenness, they
cast it all up again, and were besmeared
with filth and gore.

Darwin was so revolted that he had to reach for an apt quotation from the classical literature he had learned as a schoolboy to express his feelings:

Nam simul expletus dapibus, vinoque sepultus
Cervicem inflexam posuit, jacuitque per antrum
Immensus, saniem eructans, ac frusta cruenta
Per somnum commixta mero.

The lines are from Virgil's *Aeneid*, Book III, and describe the monstrous Cyclops, sated by the blood of his victims: "For when, gorged with the feast, and drowned in wine, the monster rested his drooping neck, and lay in endless length throughout the cave, in his sleep vomiting gore and morsels mixed with blood and wine …"

The following morning, the *mansos* set out in search of revenge. Darwin was by now entirely disgusted at the appalling savagery of the war that was being waged on the Indians, and incredulous at the indifference of those who supported the war. He concluded:

This is a dark picture: but how much more shocking is the unquestionable fact that all the women who appear above twenty years old are massacred in cold blood! When I exclaimed that this appeared rather inhuman, [my informant] answered, "Why, what can be done? they breed so!" Every one here is fully convinced that this is the most just war, because it is against barbarians. Who would believe in this age that such atrocities could be committed in a Christian civilized country?

He was glad to leave the place behind, and to see his shipmates again; though not so glad that he was ready to miss the chance of further land travel. The *Beagle* arrived on 24th August, and a week later sailed for the Plata – but Darwin was not on board.

8 September – 20 September: Bahia Blanca to Buenos Aires

FitzRoy agreed to allow Darwin to continue his overland journey as far as Buenos Aires – a distance of 400 miles across, across a hazardous war zone.

> September 18th: – I hired a Gaucho to
> accompany me on my ride to Buenos Aires,
> though with some difficulty, as the father
> of one man was afraid to let him go, and
> another, who seemed willing, was described
> to me as so fearful, that I was afraid to take
> him, for I was told that if he saw an ostrich
> at a distance, he would mistake it for an
> Indian, and would fly like the wind away ...

On the second day out, Darwin decided to climb a mountain composed mainly of white quartz rock:

> I was, on the whole, disappointed with this
> ascent ... The scene, however, was novel,
> and a little danger, like salt to meat, gave
> it a relish. That the danger was very little
> was certain, for my two companions made
> a good fire – a thing which is never done
> when it is supposed that Indians are near. I

reached the place of our bivouac by sunset,
and drinking much maté, and smoking
several cigaritos, soon made up my bed for
the night. The wind was very strong and
cold, but I never slept more comfortably.

On 16th September they reached a post-house at the foot
of the Sierra Tapalguen. Here they were told a "fact which
I would not have credited, if I had not partly ocular proof
of it; namely, that, during the previous night hail as large
as small apples, and extremely hard, had fallen with such
violence, as to kill the greater number of the wild animals".
Darwin's party recovered the bodies of 20 deer, and feasted
on this "hail-stricken meat". The following night, Darwin
dined on puma, which he said was very much like veal.

All the "Christians" they met on their journey quizzed
them eagerly about the progress of the war against the
barbarians, and Darwin found it useful to drop hints
about his friendly relations with Rosas, and to flash the
credentials Rosas had given him:

> ... on arriving at a post-house we were
> told by the owner, that if we had not a
> regular passport we must pass on, for there
> were so many robbers he would trust no
> one. When he read, however, my passport,
> which began with "El Naturalista Don
> Carlos," his respect and civility were
> as unbounded as his suspicions had been
> before. What a naturalist might be, neither
> he nor his countrymen, I suspect, had any
> idea; but probably my title lost nothing of
> its value from that cause.

Darwin arrived in Buenos Aires by noon on 20th September and rode directly to the house of Mr Lumb, an English merchant who had offered him hospitality. Darwin was impressed by the regularity of the city's layout – "every street is at right angles to the one it crosses" – and wrote that though the individual buildings had no great architectural beauty, the general effect was impressive. What did not impress him was the first bullfight he saw:

> The whole sight is horrible and revolting:
> the ground is almost made of bones; and the
> horses and riders are drenched with gore.

The former scourge of British wildlife was becoming more sensitive to the sufferings of animals, and was learning that to examine creatures was a higher pleasure than the thrill of shooting them.

27 September – 4 November: Expedition to Santa Fe and return to Montevideo

After a week of enjoying the comforts of a wealthy town, Darwin embarked on a further trip: to Santa Fe, "situated nearly three hundred English miles from Buenos Ayres, on the banks of the Parana". A few days into the trip, he had to take to his bed, suffering from a bad headache.

> Many of the remedies used by the people
> of the country are ludicrously strange, but
> too disgusting to be mentioned. One of
> the least nasty is to kill and cut open two
> puppies and bind them on each side of a
> broken limb ...

(What could the more nasty have been?) He investigated the geology, collected fossils – including mastodon bones and the fossil tooth of an extinct breed of horse, and heard tales of the terrible drought, the *gran seco*, that had afflicted the country between 1827 and 1830. Thousands upon thousands of cattle had rushed to what was left of the river Parana, became too exhausted to drag themselves back up its muddy banks, and slid down into the shallow water to perish. The carcasses rotted in the sun, and the stench made the area impassable. It made Darwin wonder what fossil record this might have left, and how archaeologists of some future date might take the mass of animal skeletons as pointing to a cataclysmic flood, "rather than to the common order of things". He was beginning to doubt the wisdom of the geological books he had read with such excitement. Geologists who had not traveled in distant lands might well have been mistaken in their assumptions. Over the five years of the circumnavigation, Darwin gradually shed his confidence in Sedgwick and Lyell, the men who had inspired him to "read" landscapes.

Illness forced Darwin to return to Montevideo by the river Parana on-board a *balandra* – a one-masted vessel weighing about a hundred tons. On 20th October, worried about the slow progress his boat was making, and anxious to reach his destination before the *Beagle* was due to sail, he went on shore at Las Conchas, only to find himself placed under arrest. A violent revolution was underway, and all the ports had been embargoed. He could neither return to his ship nor leave the port. After long negotiations with the commander, he was given permission to approach the rebel encampment: "The general, officers, and soldiers, all appeared, and I believe really were, great villains." After further arguments, Darwin discovered that dropping the name of General Rosas worked wonders, and he was told that, though he could not be issued with a passport, he would not be detained by any sentinels. Eventually, after about two weeks, he managed to escape on a packet bound for Montevideo.

4 November – 6 December: Montevideo
14–28 November: Expedition to Mercedes and return

Darwin rejoined the *Beagle* only to find that FitzRoy, busy drawing up charts, did not intend to sail for several weeks, so he took the opportunity to make his final venture of the year. On this trip, he was intrigued by the skillful way in which the Gauchos would coax their horses into swimming – they would strip naked, ride the horse into the river until it was almost out of its depth: then slide off, grab hold of its tail and urge it to swim forward by splashing water. On the far bank, they would re-mount: "A naked man on a naked horse is a fine spectacle …"

On the evening of 19th November, Darwin stopped at a large *estancia*, where he was amused to note that, despite the fact that they were prosperous (and might thus, as in most comparable societies, reasonably be expected to be well-informed), they had notions about the nature of the world that were every bit as quaint as those held by inhabitants of far more remote regions.

> They expressed, as was usual, unbounded astonishment at the globe being round, and could scarcely credit that a hole would, if deep enough, come out on the other side.

They told him that they had heard stories of a land where

there were six months of light and six months of darkness, and where the inhabitants were tall and thin. They pressed for details of how horses and cattle were reared in England, and when he assured them that English farmers did not use lassoes, they assumed that the English used nothing but the *bolas*. Then came a potentially embarrassing moment.

> The Captain at last said, he had one question to ask me, & he should be very much obliged if I would answer him with all truth. – I trembled to think how deeply scientific it would be, – "it was whether the ladies of Buenos Ayres were not the handsomest in the world." I replied, "Charmingly so." – He added, I have one other question – "do ladies in any other part of the world wear such large combs." I solemnly assured him they did not. – They were absolutely delighted. – The Captain exclaimed, "Look there, a man, who has seen half the world, says it is the case; we always thought so, but now we know it." My excellent judgement in combs and beauty procured me a most hospitable reception; the captain forced me to take his bed, & he would sleep on his Recado.

Charmed as he was by the spirit of hospitality to strangers that prevailed here, the increasingly humane Darwin was also – like many an Englishman abroad in countries which have different ways of treating other species – shocked by their callous treatment of horses.

Animals are so abundant in these countries, that humanity and self-interest are not closely united; therefore I fear it is that the former is here scarcely known. One day, riding in the Pampas with a very respectable "estanciero," my horse, being tired, lagged behind. The man often shouted at me to spur him. When I remonstrated that it was a pity, for the horse was quite exhausted, he cried out, "Why not? – never mind – spur him – it is *my* horse" I had then some difficulty in making him comprehend that it was for the horse's sake, and not on his account, that I did not choose to use my spurs. He exclaimed, with a look of great surprise "Ah, Don Carlos, que cosa!" It was clear that such an idea had never before entered his head.

Upon his return to Montevideo, Darwin took some time to reflect on his six months of meeting the locals. Though he lamented the tendency of the Gauchos to be dangerously violent, and particularly the habit of slashing each other's faces in knife fights, he otherwise concluded that they were admirable men: "The Gaucho is invariably most obliging, polite and hospitable: I did not meet with even one instance of rudeness or inhospitality." He was a little more skeptical about the town-dwellers and the educated classes. On the one hand, they were polite and dignified, and the women showed "excellent taste" in their dress; they enjoyed a free press, were tolerant of foreigners, and had shown that they would go out of their way to help anyone "professing the humblest pretensions to science". On the other, they were "stained by many vices" of which the Gauchos were free:

> Sensuality, mockery of all religion, and the grossest corruption, are far from uncommon. Nearly every public officer can be bribed.

Still, he reflected in true John Bull style:

> When speaking of these countries, the manner in which they have been brought up by their unnatural parent, Spain, should always be borne in mind. On the whole, perhaps, more credit is due for what has been done, than blame for that which may be deficient.

FitzRoy's repaired schooner, the *Adventure*, was now ready to sail with Lt Wickham as its captain. The two ships dutifully worked their way up and down the coast several times, from Port Desire down to the Straits of Magellan, making detailed surveys.

6 December: *Beagle* sailed from Rio Plata for last time

Chapter 7

*Return to Tierra del Fuego
and into the Pacific*

**23 December 1833 – 4 January 1834: Port Desire
2 February: Port Famine**

The ship's company celebrated Christmas at Port
Desire. Aware of the need to maintain morale at this
season, and recalling the miseries of the previous Christmas, FitzRoy ordered the whole crew ashore to compete
in a variety of games, including running, wrestling and
a fairly violent stunt known as "swinging the monkey",
in which a sailor was suspended upside down and spun
around as his shipmates tried to hit him. Darwin, ever the
keen-eyed marksman, made himself popular by killing a
170-pound guanaco – a cousin of the llama – which was
duly roasted and devoured for the festive lunch.

A few days after the Christmas break, they encountered the Patagonian Indians, who, thanks to the tall tales
of early explorers, had passed into maritime legend as

"giants". The crew were rather impressed by them, especially the trio who came on board the *Beagle* as FitzRoy's guests. "At tea they behaved quite like gentlemen, used a knife & fork & helped themselves with a spoon …"

In February, the *Beagle* and *Adventure* sailed down towards Tierra del Fuego. In spite of their earlier experiences, everyone was once more shocked by the appallingly primitive state of its natives. Darwin was particularly horrified at the vision of a woman sullenly and silently nursing her newborn baby while the chill rains teemed down on her and the infant.

A shock of a different kind came when they finally reached Woollya Cove in March. Three canoes came out to greet them, manned by "savages": all strangers, it seemed, until one of them made a characteristic naval salute. It was Jemmy Button. FitzRoy said that he could have wept at the sight. Darwin agreed:

> It was quite painful to behold him: thin, pale and without a remnant of clothes … I never saw so complete and grievous a change.

When he was taken on board and dressed in warm clothes, he almost immediately reverted to his old ways, and spoke politely in English. FitzRoy and Darwin suggested to him several times that they would be willing to have him back on board and eventually return him to England; but, to their surprise and dismay, he would have none of it. There was now a Mrs Button, and he was determined to stay with her. The Fuegian and the Englishmen exchanged final gifts, shook hands and bade each other farewell. They would never meet again.

5 March: Sailed from Tierra del Fuego
10 March – 7 April: East Falkland Island

There had been more unpleasantness on the Falklands in the crew's absence. A group of Gauchos and Indians, led by one Antonio Rivero, had murdered several British subjects and some Spaniards. The Navy had sent in a party of five armed sailors led by a lieutenant, who had successfully rounded up all the killers save Rivero. The fugitive was hiding out on Berkeley Sound.

The lieutenant, now acting as Governor, asked Fitz-Roy for his assistance. The captain duly sent out a force of marines who captured Rivero and put him in irons in the hold of the *Beagle*. Darwin approved, but he was also critical of the incompetence and half-hearted nature of British policy on the Falklands, which had been left with no protection against such acts of violence.

There was also good reason to be cheerful. The same ship that had brought the five sailors had also brought the latest consignment of mail from England. Charles devoured all the gossip from his family; he was even more delighted by a letter from Henslow, who told him that all of his specimens had made it safely back to England, and that the name of Charles Darwin was already becoming famous. The megatherium fossils had been exhibited to the nation's leading scholars at a Cambridge meeting of the British Association for the Advancement of Science, and had impressed them all. Henslow urged him to find as many more fossils as he could, and begged him not to leave the mission early.

For Darwin, this was a turning point. Until now, his pleasure in the adventure of exploring and collecting had been compromised by his worry that he was really no more than, as he put it, "a sort of Jackall, a lions provider". Henslow's words made it clear that he was now seen as a true Naturalist, accepted and even admired by the men he considered his betters. For the next few weeks he set about his geological and biological tasks in a frenzy of delight.

18 April – 8 May: Expedition up the Santa Cruz River
1–8 June: Port Famine
10 June: Sailed for last time from Tierra del Fuego
28 June – 13 July: Chiloe Island

On 12th May 1834, the *Beagle*, accompanied by *Adventure*, set off for the Straits of Magellan. It was one of the crew's most uncomfortable journeys: they endured weeks of heavy snow and temperatures well below freezing. On 10th June, as they passed through the Straits of Magellan, Darwin looked at the jagged shoreline with trepidation:

> One sight of such a coast is enough to
> make a landsman dream for a week about
> shipwrecks, peril, and death; and with this
> sight we bade farewell for ever to Tierra
> del Fuego.

At last they made it to the Pacific. Their next destination, Valparaiso, was 1,700 miles to the north, and the *Beagle's* passage up the Chilean coastline was slowed by severe gales. During this leg of the journey, the ship's purser, Mr Rowlett, died after a short illness: "the funeral service was read on the quarter deck, and his body lowered into the sea; it is an aweful and solemn sound that splash of the waters over the body of an old ship-mate." After about a thousand miles, the *Beagle* was forced by severe storms to put in to shore at the large island of Chiloe, where it remained for two weeks – long enough for Charles to make some expeditions into the island's forests.

23 July: Arrived at Valparaiso

A further seven hundred miles brought the crew to Valparaiso on 23rd July 1834, where they would stay for three months, repairing the ship and drawing up charts. Everyone's spirits lifted at once:

> The Beagle anchored late at night in the bay of Valparaiso, the chief seaport of Chile. When morning came, everything appeared delightful. After Tierra del Fuego, the climate felt delicious – the atmosphere so dry, and the heavens so clear and blue with the sun shining brightly, that all nature seemed sparkling with life. The view from the anchorage is very pretty ...

Shortly after arriving, Darwin made contact with Richard Corfield (1804–97), an old school friend from Shrewsbury. Corfield, who was working as a merchant in the city, offered Darwin the use of his house as a base. Darwin accepted, and was grateful: "He is as hospitable & kind in deed as a Spaniard is in professions, – than which I can say no more. It is most pleasant to meet with such a straitforward thorough Englishman, as Corfield is, in these vile countries." After relaxing for two weeks – the idlest he had been since leaving home – he felt the tug of geology. On 14th August he set out with local guides on a six-week trek on horseback, making geological surveys of the foothills of the Andes. Darwin was in high good humor.

> The setting of the sun was glorious; the
> valleys being black while the snowy peaks
> of the Andes yet retained a ruby tint. When
> it was dark, we made a fire beneath a
> little arbour of bamboos, fried our charqui
> (or dried slips of beef), took our maté,
> and were quite comfortable. There is an
> inexpressible charm in thus living in the
> open air ...

Yet he was not so pleased with his Chilean traveling companions: "The Guasos of Chile, who correspond to the Gauchos of the Pampas are, however, a very different set of beings." Darwin observed that the Guasos were much more deferential to him than his friends on the Pampas. Their behavior led him to speculate about the different social orders of the two countries: Chile, being "the more civilized of the two countries", had an aristocracy of wealth, and a dramatic "inequality of riches". Travelers in Argentina, as he had noticed, would be treated with great hospitality by the poorest of folk; Chileans would also allow a traveler to stay with them for the night, but they would expect to be paid. Darwin summed up the difference in a pungent sentence:

> The Gaucho, though he may be a
> cutthroat, is a gentleman; the Guaso is in a
> few respects better, but at the same time a
> vulgar, ordinary fellow.

They pressed on, meeting locals on the way. Darwin was

often as interested in the local architecture and customs as he was in the stones and flora – a curiosity which some found offensive. On 5th September he had to justify his ways:

> In the evening we reached a comfortable farm-house, where there were several very pretty senoritas. They were much horrified at my having entered one of their churches out of mere curiosity. They asked me, "Why do you not become a Christian – for our religion is certain?" I assured them that I was a sort of Christian, but they would not hear of it – appealing to my own words, "Do not your padres, your very bishops, marry?" The absurdity of a bishop having a wife particularly struck them: they scarcely knew whether to be most amused or horror-struck by such an enormity.

Darwin pushed on, working hard every day, until, at the end of September, he started to feel seriously ill from some kind of gastric infection. He blamed it on having swilled some "sour new-made wine"; whatever the cause, it made him vomit and gave him stomach aches – exactly the symptoms that would plague him later in life. Eventually he was forced to hire a carriage to take him back to Corfield's house, where he rested and was treated by Mr Bynoe, the new surgeon of the *Beagle*, with generous quantities of castor oil. Apart from the odd bout of fever, this was the first major episode of ill health in his life. On 30th October he wrote to his sister Caroline:

> I find being sick at stomach inclines one
> also to be home-sick. I suspect we will
> pay T. del Fuego another visit; but of
> this good Lord deliver us: it is kept very
> secret, lest the men should desert; every
> one so hates the confounded country. Our
> voyage sounded much more delightful in
> the instructions, than it really is.

If Darwin was gloomy, his Captain was in despair. After about a month in the city, FitzRoy received a communication from the Admiralty. It was bad news. Their Lordships had refused his request for a retrospective approval of his actions, and would not reimburse him for the money he had spent buying and repairing the *Adventure*. He had no alternative but to sell it, at a much lower price than he had paid. This was a severe blow to his personal fortune, but a worse one to his mind and emotional stability. He plunged into one of his depressions, and for the next two months suffered what amounted to a nervous breakdown, from which he could not drag himself free.

FitzRoy's condition alarmed Charles, who noted that the captain had become "thin & unwell" and even feared for his sanity:

> This was accompanied by a morbid
> depression of spirits, & a loss of all decision
> & resolution. The captain was afraid that his
> mind was becoming deranged (being aware
> of his hereditary disposition). All that Bynoe
> could say, that it was merely the effect of
> bodily health and exhaustion after such
> application, would not do; he invalided &

Wickham was appointed to the command.

FitzRoy's decision to declare himself unfit for command prompted Darwin to resolve that he would also quit the *Beagle*, continue his explorations of the Andes alone and then head back to England via Buenos Aires. Fortunately, Wickham managed to persuade FitzRoy not only to take back his command, but to cancel his idea of one last trip to Tierra del Fuego. Everyone, not least Darwin, was immensely relieved.

10 November: Sailed for Chiloe Island
21 November – 4 February 1835: Chiloe Island

The voyagers left Valparaiso on 10 November 1834 and headed back southwards to explore their former shelter, the island of Chiloe, and about 250 miles of the Chilean coast, down at Cap Tres Montes. The *Beagle* was to explore the west coast of the island while a boat party made a survey of the east coast. The second team set off in two small boats under the command of a junior officer, Sullivan; Darwin was with them. Everyone seemed to enjoy it – as Darwin wrote to his sisters:

> We had a remarkably pleasant boat
> journey along the Eastern Coast. You
> cannot imagine what merry work such a
> wandering journey is: in the morning we
> never know where we shall sleep at night.
> Carrying, like snail, our houses with us we
> are always independent; when the day is
> over we sit round our fire and pity all you
> who are confined within houses.

Darwin rejoined the *Beagle* at their rendezvous point on the southern coast; Sullivan and the others carried on until 18th January 1885. The *Beagle* made its way through the Chonos archipelago, battered by gales, until on 20th December they finally reached Cap Tres Montes and turned the ship northwards once more.

A few days later, the crew spotted a man on the shoreline, frantically waving a shirt to catch their attention. FitzRoy sent a rescue boat, and the sailors discovered that this figure was an American sailor who had deserted a whaling boat with five of his shipmates to escape ill-treatment by a tyrannical captain. The deserters had made a successful escape in a small boat by night, only to find themselves caught in dangerous waters. Their boast was smashed on the rocks, leaving them as castaways, living on almost nothing but raw shellfish and meat from the occasional seal they managed to kill. They had been trapped for fifteen months when they had the good fortune to spot the *Beagle*.

On 18th January 1835 the *Beagle* made it back to San Carlos on Chiloe, where it was joined by Sullivan and his boat party.

What happened next was utterly unexpected.

Chapter 8

Earthquakes and Volcanoes

22 November 1835 – 8 January: Expedition from San Carlos to Cucao and return
18–22 February: Valdivia
4–6 March: Concepcion
11 March: Valparaiso

Throughout their surveys on Chiloe, the men of the *Beagle* had all noticed that one of the high mountains they could see off in the distance, Mount Orsono, had begun "spouting out volumes of smoke". It was obvious that an eruption was coming; and when it came, Darwin, using FitzRoy's telescope, declared it

> a very magnificent sight ... by the aid of a glass, in the midst of the great red glare of light, dark objects might be seen to be thrown up and fall down ...

After the hard work and soakings on Chiloe, it was a great relief to stop for a while at the small coastal town of Valdivia. Here Darwin shopped, made short trips into the nearby hills, and attended a ball. The future author of a volume on the expression of emotion in men and animals was intrigued to notice that the women of Valdivia, unlike their sisters on Chiloe, had the ability to blush when they flirted.

Then came the single most dramatic day of the voyage. On the evening of 20th February 1835, Darwin wrote:

> This day has been memorable in the annals of Valdivia, for the most severe earthquake experienced by the oldest inhabitant. I happened to be on shore, and was lying down in the wood to rest myself. It came on suddenly, and lasted two minutes, but the time appeared much longer. The rocking of the ground was very sensible.... There was no difficulty in standing upright, but the motion made me almost giddy: it was something like the movement of a vessel in a little cross-ripple, or still more like that felt by a person skating on thin ice, which bends under the weight of his body.

Since most of the local houses were modest in scale and made of wood, the damage was not too bad. But when they sailed on to Concepcion, 200 miles to the north, they found a scene of almost total devastation. Not a single house had been left habitable – there was "nothing more than piles & lines of bricks, tiles & timbers". Though only a hundred or so had been killed by falling masonry during the quake itself, the subsequent tidal waves took the lives of others, and added to the chaos. The place had collapsed into anarchy: "Those who had saved any property were obliged to keep a constant watch, for thieves prowled about, and at each little trembling of the ground, with one hand they beat their breasts and cried 'Misericordia!' and then with the other filched what they could from the ruins ..."

Darwin was overwhelmed by the sight; fascinated, too:

> To my mind since leaving England we have
> scarcely beheld any one other sight so deeply
> interesting. The Earthquake and Volcano
> are parts of one of the greatest phenomena
> to which the world is subject.

He expanded on this sentiment in a letter to his sister Caroline: the devastation wrought by the earthquake was

> The most awful [i.e., awe-inspiring]
> spectacle I ever beheld ... The force of the
> shock must have been immense, the ground is
> traversed by rents, the solid rock is shivered
> ... it is one of the three most interesting
> spectacles I have beheld since leaving
> England – a Fuegian savage. – Tropical
> Vegetation – and the ruins of Concepcion.

Darwin's orthodox ideas about the stability of the earth's surface were at once overthrown. He wrote to Henslow:

> I wish some of the Geologists who think the
> Earthquakes of these times are trifling could
> see the way the solid rock is shivered ...

For the rest of his time in Chile, Darwin's mind raced as he pondered the implications of his experience.

14–18 March: Santiago
18 March – 10 April: To Mendoza
10–15 April: Santiago
15–27 April: Return to Valparaiso
27 April – 5 July: To Coquimbo and Copiapo

The *Beagle* sailed back to the comforts of Valparaiso. Once ashore, Charles left his crewmates and headed across land to the Chilean capital, Santiago. Then he organized his next adventure: a hazardous crossing of the Andes. Yet again, he found the experience exhilarating:

> It was something more than enjoyment:
> I cannot express the delight which I felt
> at such a famous winding up of all my
> Geology in South America. I literally
> could hardly sleep at nights for thinking
> over my day's work. The scenery was
> so new & so majestic; everything at an
> elevation of 12,000 ft. bears so different
> an aspect from that in a lower country. I
> have seen many views more beautiful, but
> none with so strongly marked a character.
> To a Geologist also there are such manifest
> proofs of excessive violence; the strata of
> the highest pinnacles are tossed about like
> the crust of a broken pie.

Refitted, the *Beagle* sailed north from Valparaiso. Darwin traveled by land, carrying out yet further investigations

– of local mines as well as rocks, and rejoined the ship at the port of Coquimbo – a couple of hundred miles north of Valpariso. Coquimbo was a town of about 8,000 inhabitants which was, Darwin thought, "remarkable for nothing but its extreme quietness". The quiet did not last. Here, he experienced a second earthquake. Darwin was at dinner with a hospitable English resident, Mr Edwards, when it happened:

> I heard the forecoming rumble, but from
> the screams of the ladies, the running of the
> servants, and the rush of several gentlemen
> to the doorway, I could not distinguish the
> motion. Some of the women afterwards
> were crying with terror and one gentleman
> said he should not be able to sleep all night,
> or if he did, it would only be to dream of
> falling houses.

19 July – 6 September: Callao and Lima

In mid-July, the crew anchored at Iquique, but found it in a state of war: four "chiefs in arms" were battling it out with guns for control of the place, The travelers moved on to Lima, which in some respects was even worse. Darwin noted that it was in "a wretched state of decay: the streets are nearly unpaved; and heaps of filth are piled up in all directions, where the black gallinazos, tame as poultry, pick up bits of carrion …" But this unpleasant first impression was misleading: Darwin found the citizens of Lima hospitable and intelligent, and he was very impressed by the fashion sense of the elegant ladies of the town, who wore black elasticated gowns and veils that were worn so as to leave only one eye uncovered: "But then that one eye is so black and brilliant and has such powers of motion and expression that its effect was very powerful." Years later, while working on *The Descent of Man*, Darwin spent thousands of hours pondering the importance of decoration in the reproductive activities of many animals, including *homo sapiens*.

Darwin rejoined the *Beagle*, and it set sail from South American waters on 7th September.

It was the beginning of the long journey home.

Chapter 9

Galapagos

15 September – 20 October: Galapagos Islands

The next port of call came into view on 15th September 1835: the southernmost island of the archipelago sometimes known as the *Islas Encantadas*, or "Enchanted Islands", but more commonly as the Galapagos. With the benefit of almost two centuries of hindsight, we can now see clearly that this was the part of the voyage which brought Darwin closest to discovering the mechanism by which species evolve; but while he was there, he was only just beginning to turn such matters over in his mind. Contrary to some popular legends, Darwin did not have a sudden, blinding vision of the truth of evolution in the Galapagos. It was only several years later, pondering his notes and specimens back in England, that the significance of what he had witnessed slowly and inevitably grew on him. But he did come tantalizingly close:

> The natural history of these islands is
> eminently curious, and well deserves
> attention. Most of the organic productions
> are aboriginal creations, found nowhere
> else; there is even a difference between
> the inhabitants of the different islands;
> yet all show a marked relationship with
> those of America, though separated from
> that continent by an open space of ocean,
> between 500 and 600 miles in width ...

Moreover, he had noticed:

> ....by far the most remarkable feature in the
> natural history of this archipelago; it is,
> that the different islands to a considerable
> extent are inhabited by a different set of
> beings ...

But why? It seemed to defy common sense. Darwin was
puzzled, excited, even awed:

> ... it is the circumstance, that several of
> the islands possess their own species of
> the tortoise, mocking-thrush, finches, and
> numerous plants, these species having the
> same general habits, occupying analogous
> situations, and obviously filling the same
> place in the natural economy of this
> archipelago, that strikes me with wonder.

He summed up his sense of being on the edge of a grand revelation in one extraordinary, so-near-and-yet-so-far sentence:

> Hence, both in space and time, we seem
> to be brought somewhat near to that great
> fact – that mystery of mysteries – the first
> appearance of new beings on this earth.

Though the full meaning of his observations remained latent, the islands nonetheless were a magnificent treasure-store for any naturalist. "Galapagos" is the Spanish word for "tortoise", and Darwin soon saw the reason for this name:

> As I was walking along I met two
> large tortoises, each of which must have
> weighed at least two hundred pounds:
> one was eating a piece of cactus, and as
> I approached, it stared at me and slowly
> walked away: the other gave a deep hiss
> and drew in its head. These huge reptiles,
> surrounded by the black lava, the leafless
> shrubs, and large cacti, appeared to my
> fancy like some antediluvian animals.

On James Island (so named by early seventeenth-century English explorers in honor of their King) the men of the *Beagle* fell in with a party of "Spaniards", who had come to dry fish and salt tortoise meat. Throughout this venture, the Englishmen subsisted "entirely on tortoise-meat: the breast-plate roasted (as the Gauchos do *carne con cuero*), with the flesh on it, is very good. and the young tortoises make excellent soup; but otherwise the meat to my taste is indifferent."

They sailed westwards again on 20th October 1835, setting course for Tahiti, 3,200 miles away.

15–26 November: Tahiti

During the three weeks or so of their voyage to Tahiti, both Darwin and FitzRoy took advantage of this unusual period of enforced leisure to open some of the books on the South Seas that had been standing neglected on the shelves of the Captain's cabin. The weather was hot, but not unpleasantly so: FitzRoy permitted some relaxation in the ship's dress code, and a holiday spirit prevailed. In the warm evenings he and Darwin would sit up on deck, dine on the turtle meat they had brought from the Galapagos, and share the discoveries they had made during that day's reading.

FitzRoy, the quiet evangelist, was most interested in what they would discover about the work of missionaries in the countries that lay ahead of them. The last substantial writer on Tahiti, Otto von Kotzebue – a well-known Russian explorer of the day – had described the effect of English missionaries as a cultural disaster: they had, he claimed, ruined the Tahitians' traditional cheerfulness, thrown their weight around, fired up dissension. This was uncomfortable reading for one who still, despite the disappointments of Tierra del Fuego, placed faith in the missionary movement. Darwin, for his part, was most curious to see if the Tahitians still showed the innocent, unrestrained sexuality about which his grandfather Erasmus had written so enthusiastically.

The *Beagle* reached Tahiti at dawn on 15th November, and was at once surrounded by canoes full of welcoming Tahitians. The gestures of hospitality grew warmer:

> After dinner, we landed to enjoy all the
> delights produced by the first impression

of a new country, and that country
the charming Tahiti. A crowd of men,
women, and children, was collected on the
memorable point Venus, ready to receive
us with laughing, merry faces.

Otto von Kotzebue had obviously been a prejudiced witness. Darwin was utterly delighted by these people, and was moved by their generosity, gentle manners and rare beauty:

There is a mildness in the expression of
their countenances which at once banishes
the idea of a savage ... They are very
tall, broad-shouldered, athletic and well-
proportioned ... A white man bathing by the
side of a Tahitian, was like a plant bleached
by the gardener's art compared with a fine
dark green one growing vigorously in the
open fields.

Darwin recruited a couple of Tahitian men to accompany him on his explorations of the forests. When the time came to bivouac, he was as impressed by the natives' various practical skills as he had been by their good looks. His two companions swiftly fashioned a shelter using banana leaves as thatch and bamboo shoots as rafters, all held together with strips of tree bark. They made comfortable beds from withered leaves, and cooked a delicious evening meal by wrapping beef, fish, bananas and other food-stuffs in leaves and then placing them between two layers of stones, heated in the campfire and then covered with earth. They washed down this hot food with cool water from coconut shells. It was a sharp contrast to the ugliness and uselessness of the inhabitants of Tierra del Fuego.

> I did indeed admire this scene, when I compared it with an uncultivated one in the temperate zones. I felt the force of the observation that man, at least savage man, with his reasoning powers only partly developed, is the child of the tropics.

The *Beagle*'s Tahitian idyll ended with some diplomacy between Captain FitzRoy and the Queen of Tahiti over the tricky matter of a fine of three thousand dollars that was being demanded of her country by the British government in compensation for an attack on a vessel sailing under the Union Jack ("I cannot sufficiently express our general surprise at the extreme good sense, the reasoning powers, moderation, candour, and prompt resolution, which were displayed on all sides"). This was followed, the next day, by a festive reception for the Queen and her entourage on board the *Beagle*. The Tahitians enjoyed a display of fireworks, and the singing of the ship's company; though the Queen wryly observed that she did not think the more boisterous of their songs could possibly be a hymn.

The following evening, with a gentle land-breeze behind them, the *Beagle*'s course was set west and south, towards New Zealand. In a journey largely made up of hard work, harsh discipline, discomforts and dangers, Tahiti had been a short vacation in Paradise. They left with regret.

Chapter 10

Slow Journey Home

21–30 December: Bay of Islands, New Zealand

The *Beagle* arrived at the coast of New Zealand on 19th December 1835. Darwin was not at all impressed, either by the natives – whom he found ugly, filthy, hostile and potentially dangerous – or by most of the English settlers, who struck him as drunken, shiftless and lawless. Those who now think of Darwin as a militant atheist will be surprised to hear that the one thing that gave him cause for hope in New Zealand was the conduct and the accomplishments of the Christian missionaries. Darwin spent the Christmas period in an English-style farmhouse run by missionaries in the remote settlement of Waimate. After the dirt and desolation that had so depressed him elsewhere in the country, he was captivated by the fine crops, the abundant and varied fruits, vegetables and flowers, the stables, the water-mill and the forge.

> All of this is very surprising, when it is
> considered that five years ago nothing but
> the fern flourished here. Moreover, native
> workmanship, taught by the missionaries,
> has effected this change; – the lesson of the
> missionary is the enchanter's wand.

He was no less struck and pleased by the native New Zealanders (the word "Maori" was not then in general use) who had been converted: he enjoyed watching the young boys playing a game of cricket with the missionaries' son, "very merry and good-humoured", and was charmed by the house-maids: "Their clean, tidy and healthy appearance, like that of the dairy-maids in England, formed a wonderful contrast with the women of the filthy hovels in Kororadika." His most cherished impression was of a group of Maori children sitting around a table for their Christmas tea:

> I never saw a nicer or more merry group;
> and to think that this was in the centre of
> the land of cannibalism, murder, and all
> atrocious crimes!

It was an uplifting sight, and it gave Darwin cause for optimism that the progress of Christianity among the natives might eventually create a civil and prosperous nation on "this fine island". Nonetheless:

> I believe we were all glad to leave New
> Zealand. It is not a pleasant place. Amongst
> the natives there is absent that charming
> simplicity which is found in Tahiti; and

the greater part of the English are the very
refuse of society.

12 January: Sydney Cove, New South Wales, Australia
16–27 January: Expedition to Blue Mountains,
Bathurst and Dunheved
28–29 January: Sydney
5–17 February: Tasmania
6–14 March: King George's Sound

The next stop was Sydney, where the voyagers put into
harbor on 12th January 1836. Australia, Darwin immediately concluded, was superior to New Zealand in almost
every respect: in just 48 years, Sydney had grown from a
minimal settlement into a thriving, well-ordered city of
23,000 souls. Darwin seldom waxed patriotic in *Voyage
of the Beagle*, but the handsomeness and prosperity of the
city ("a fine town") brought out his inner John Bull:

> It is a most magnificent testimony to the
> power of the British nation. Here, in a
> less promising country, scores of years
> have done many times more than an
> equal number of centuries have effected
> in South America. My first feeling was
> to congratulate myself that I was born an
> Englishman.

Yet he was not a narrow-minded jingoist even in those
days when nostalgic love of his native land (he was by now
longing to be home again) waxed most intense. Charles
was also favorably impressed by a group of Aboriginals
whom he met on a riding tour. A few of them spoke a little

English, and he enjoyed their company:

> ... their countenances were good-humoured
> and pleasant and they appeared far from
> such utterly degraded beings as usually
> represented. In their own arts they are
> admirable; a cap being fixed at thirty yards
> distance, they transfixed it with the spear
> delivered by the throwing stick, with the
> rapidity of an arrow from the bow of a
> practised Archer; in tracking animals and
> men they show the most wonderful sagacity.

The longer he stayed in the country, though, the less sure Darwin became about the new society that was emerging here. He lamented the way in which the arrival of white Europeans had brought about a drastic decrease in the aboriginal population, thanks to imported diseases, alcohol and the extermination of many wild animals. He feared that the native Australians were themselves doomed to extinction, and expressed his concern in words which anticipate the much later formulation, "survival of the fittest":

> The varieties of man seem to act on each
> other in the same way as different species
> of animals – the stronger always extirpating
> the weaker.

Darwin participated in a kangaroo hunt and was disappointed not to encounter any, though he did manage to catch a "potaroo", or rat kangaroo – his first encounter with a marsupial. The curiosity of such animals tempted him towards blasphemous thought: they were so distinct from the mammals he knew in England that "An unbeliever ... might exclaim ... 'Surely two distinct Creators must have been at work'." During an evening stroll, he was fascinated and delighted "to see several of the famous Ornithorhyncus paradoxus" – the scientific term for the duck-billed platypus: "They were diving and playing about the surface of the water, but showed so little of their bodies that they might easily be mistaken for water-rats."

He lay down by the water's edge and mused on their sheer oddity: mammals with so many of the attributes of birds. His local companion killed one of the beasts and handed the corpse to Darwin. Darwin considered it "wonderful". Perhaps, he speculated wildly, there had been three Creators, or even more? But his fundamental faith in the truth of Christian revelation was strengthened by the reassuring sight of an Australian ant-lion, a predator which threw out small bursts of sand to drive victims into its jaws, just as the sand-lions of Europe did. Thousands of miles apart, insects behaved in precisely the same way as each other. One Creator presided over Creation, after all.

On the whole, Darwin's experience of the country's geology and wildlife was more stimulating than his ventures into its society. Despite the attractions of Australia as a place where hard work was almost inevitably rewarded by prosperity, he found the tensions between the classes of convicts, freed convicts and voluntary immigrants disagreeable: "The whole community is rancorously divided ..." He concluded that "nothing but rather sharp necessity should compel me to emigrate". Years later, in middle age and with a large family to support, he changed his mind somewhat, and when the value of his investments in gold began to decline, he thought seriously about returning to a country where hard work seemed always to result in prosperity. But he was too settled in his ways: he never returned.

The *Beagle*'s Australian adventure ended with a sail south to Hobart, Tasmania; and then to King George's Sound at the south-western tip of Australia, where the crew watched a grand "corrobory", or dancing-party, illuminated by large bonfires: "a perfect display of a festival amongst the lowest barbarians."

Darwin composed a downbeat speech of leave-taking:

> Farewell, Australia! You are a rising infant and doubtless some day will reign a great princess in the south: but you are too great and ambitious for affection, yet not great enough for respect. I leave your shores without sorrow or regret.

1–12 April: Keeling Islands
29 April – 9 May: Isle of France (Mauritius)
31 May: Cape of Good Hope
8–15 June: Visits with Herschel and others

On 1st April, the *Beagle* caught sight of the Cocos Islands, also known as the Keeling Islands – a set of coral atolls in the Indian Ocean about six hundred miles from the coast of Sumatra. Its principal inhabitants comprised a hundred or so former Malay slaves and their children; and also an English gentleman, Mr Liesk, who came out to greet the *Beagle* in his boat. The Keeling Islands produced little in the way of nutritious and exportable crops save for the cocoa-nut trees that grew everywhere. Darwin was much taken by the Malays, and especially the women: "I liked both their general expressions and the sound of their voices. They appeared poor, and their houses were destitute of furniture: but it was evident, from the plumpness of the little children, that cocoa-nuts and turtle afford no bad sustenance."

The principal event of their short stay was a "Spoon Dance" – a strange ritual in which two women carried a giant spoon – a kind of puppet, dressed up in clothes – to the grave of a dead man and danced with it. The onlookers, all women and children, all sang a song to which the two women swayed; they made the Spoon-puppet convulse as if possessed by the spirit of the full moon. Darwin was not moved. "It was a most foolish spectacle, but Mr Liesk maintained that many of the Malays believed in its spiritual movements."

The *Beagle* sailed out of the lagoon on the morning of 12th April, and reached Mauritius about two weeks later. Darwin had read in various sources that the island was famous for its beauty, and he was not disappointed:

> The whole island, with its sloping border
> and central mountains, was adorned with
> an air of perfect elegance: the scenery, if
> I may use such an expression, appeared to
> the sight harmonious.

He also took keen pleasure in exploring the town, which "is of considerable size, and is said to contain 20,000 inhabitants":

> Although the island has been so many
> years under the English Government, the
> character of the place is quite French:
> indeed, I should think that Calais or

> Boulogne was much more Anglified. There
> is a very pretty little theatre, in which
> operas are excellently performed. We were
> also surprised at seeing large booksellers'
> shops, with well-stocked shelves; – music
> and reading bespeak our approach to the
> old world of civilization; for in truth both
> Australia and America are new worlds.

Darwin also found good cause to respect the Indians who
had been sent here as convicts by the administrators of
the British Raj. Some of them had been exiled for serious crimes such as murder, but many others had done
nothing worse than refuse to follow certain English laws
because of religious scruples. All of them were made to
do public works: "Before seeing these people, I had no
idea that the inhabitants of India were such noble figures
… These men are generally quiet and well-conducted;
from their outward conduct, their cleanliness, and faithful
observance of their strange religious rites, it was impossible to look at them with the same eyes as on our wretched
convicts in New South Wales." On 5th May, Charles rode
an elephant "in true Indian fashion. The circumstance
which surprised me most was its quite noiseless step." By
this time, he was already beginning to fall in love with the
place: "How pleasant it would be to pass one's life in such
quiet abodes …"

   But the tug of England was stronger. During the final
stages of the journey, his homesickness became almost
unbearable.

> For the last year, I have been wishing to
> return & have uttered my wishes in no

gentle murmurs; but now I feel inclined
to keep up one steady deep growl from
morning to night. – I count & recount
every stage in the journey homewards & an
hour lost is reckoned of more consequence
than a week formerly.

The travelers' last major stop was a two-week stay in South Africa. Darwin hardly mentions it in *Voyage of the Beagle* ("… calling at the Cape of Good Hope …"). FitzRoy's plan was to take chronometrical readings at the British observatory, and also to consult with Sir John Herschel, the most eminent of British astronomers, who was in South Africa for a four-year mission to examine the southern skies, from 1834–8. Darwin made his inevitable forays in search of animals, though this time he met with relatively little success.

But he was thrilled at meeting Herschel, who had long been one of his scientific heroes, and he was touched by Herschel's humility and even social awkwardness. This great man, he said, "never talked much, but every word which he uttered was worth listening to. He was very shy and often had a distressed expression." They discussed the recent writings of Lyell, which came very close indeed to proposing a natural rather than divine cause for the origins of life on earth. Herschel, a more devout Christian than Charles, was dismayed by this tendency. Darwin, his own views on the subject still not fully thought through, concluded that it was best not to disagree openly with his distinguished host and maintained a tactful silence

The *Beagle* set sail into the Atlantic in the middle of June.

8–14 July: St Helena
19–23 July: Ascension Island
1–6 August: Bahia, Brazil
12–17 August: Pernambuco, Brazil
4 September: St Jago
20–24 September: Azores

The next landfall was Napoleon's island of exile, St Helena, where he died in 1821. Charles "obtained lodgings within a stone's throw of Napoleon's tomb", but he disdained writing about it, feeling that the subject had already been done to death.

> After the volumes of eloquence which have
> poured forth on the subject, it is dangerous
> even to mention the tomb. A modern
> traveller, in twelve lines, burdens the poor
> little island with the following titles, – it
> is a grave, tomb, pyramid, cemetery,
> sepulchre, catacomb, sarcophagus, minaret,
> and mausoleum!

Five days after leaving St Helena, the *Beagle* reached Ascension Island:

> The only inhabitants are marines, and some
> negroes liberated from slave-ships, who
> are paid and victualled by the government.
> There is not a private person on the
> island. Many of the marines appeared well
> contented with their situation; they think it
> better to serve their one-and-twenty years
> on shore, let it be what it may, than in a

ship; in this choice, if I were a marine, I
should most heartily agree.

From Ascension Island, the *Beagle* should have sailed
north, towards England. But FitzRoy set a course west-
south-west, back to Bahia on the coast of Brazil. The
Captain's intense perfectionism made him determined,
no matter how much the crew groaned – and groan they
did – to postpone the final leg of the journey until he
had made further checks of his chronometrical readings.
They stayed for just four days. Curiously, this unexpected
detour inspired Darwin to write the most lyrical passage
in his whole book.

> While quietly walking along the shady
> pathways, and admiring each successive
> view, I wished to find language to express
> my ideas. Epithet after epithet was found
> too weak to convey to those who have not
> visited the intertropical regions, the sense
> of delight which the mind experiences. I
> have said that the plants in a hothouse fail to
> communicate a just idea of the vegetation,
> yet I must recur to it. The land is one
> great wild, untidy, luxuriant hothouse,
> made by Nature for herself, but taken
> possession of by Man, who has studded it
> with gay houses and formal gardens. How
> great would be the desire in every admirer
> of nature to behold, if such were possible,
> the scenery of another planet! yet to every
> person in Europe, it may be truly said, that
> at the distance of only a few degrees from

his native soil, the glories of another world
are opened up to him. In my last walk, I
stopped again and again to gaze on those
beauties, and endeavoured to fix forever in
my mind an impression, which at the time
I knew, sooner or later must fail. The form
of the orange-tree, the cocoa-nut, the palm,
the mango, the tree-fern, the banana, will
remain clear and separate; but the thousand
beauties which unite these into one perfect
scene must fade away: yet they will leave,
like a tale heard in childhood, a picture full
of indistinct, but most beautiful figures.

On 6th August, FitzRoy gave orders to set off in a home-
ward direction. They met with bad luck – storms blew
up and forced them to take shelter on 12th August in the
coastal town of Pernambuco: "The town is in all parts
disgusting, the streets being narrow, ill-paved, and filthy;
the houses, tall and gloomy …" It was the end of the
rainy season, and much of the surrounding country was
flooded, so Darwin could not take his usual walks. He was
also far from charmed by the locals, who were unexpectedly rude, and was quite sure about the reasons for their
bad manners:

I must here commemorate what happened
for the first time during our nearly five years
of wandering, namely, having met with a
want of politeness. I was refused in a sullen
manner at two different houses, and obtained
with difficulty from a third, permission to
pass through their gardens to an uncultivated

hill, for the purpose of viewing the country.
I feel glad that this happened in the land
of the Brazilians, for I bear them no good
will – a land also of slavery, and therefore of
moral debasement. A Spaniard would have
felt ashamed at the very thought of refusing
such a request, or of behaving to a stranger
with rudeness.

On 21st August the *Beagle* crossed the Equator, and on 9th September the Tropic of Cancer. The crew re-provisioned in the Azores and on 25th September sailed for England. Darwin's joy at the prospect of being home again was compromised by yet another bout of seasickness, since the waters were angry.

2 October: Falmouth

On 2nd October 1836, the *Beagle* docked at Falmouth: "at Falmouth I left the Beagle, having lived on board the good little vessel nearly five years."

This was not quite accurate. Like Odysseus, Darwin had spent a good part of his travels on land – of the five years he was away from home, three years and a month were spent ashore. He was never at sea for longer than 47 days at a stretch – a period of about one to three weeks was more normal – and his total time as a mariner only added up to about eighteen months.

It is striking that, when he came to write up his diaries, Darwin chose to end with observations not about the natural world, but about human nature. Though he had learned a great deal about species both living and extinct, the species about and from which he had learned most was *homo sapiens.* For all the pains he had suffered, of which seasickness was the worst:

> ... I have too deeply enjoyed the voyage,
> not to recommend any naturalist, although
> he must not expect to be so fortunate in
> his companions as I have been, to take
> all chances, and to start, on travels by
> land if possible, if otherwise, on a long
> voyage. He may feel assured, he will
> meet with no difficulties or dangers,
> excepting in rare cases, nearly so bad as
> he beforehand anticipates. In a moral point
> of view, the effect ought to be, to teach
> him good-humoured patience, freedom
> from selfishness, the habit of acting for
> himself, and of making the best of every
> occurrence. In short, he ought to partake
> of the characteristic qualities of most sailors.
> Travelling ought also to teach him distrust;
> but at the same time he will discover, how
> many truly kind-hearted people there are,
> with whom he never before had, or ever
> again will have any further communication,
> who yet are ready to offer him the most
> disinterested assistance.

Two long days of travel by coach brought Darwin back to Shrewsbury. He arrived at The Mount late at night on 4th October. The entire family was asleep, so he went straight to bed without waking them. He rose in time to join them as they were about to sit down for breakfast on the morning of 5th October. He had been away for five years and three days.

Startled by this unheralded appearance, his father burst out: "Why, the shape of his head is quite altered!"

Epilogue

T he rest of the story has been told many times. Once settled back in the United Kingdom, Darwin never left its shores again. Indeed, once he had settled in his country house in Kent, he seldom left home save to take water cures for his dreadful stomach pains in Malvern, or to consult his brother scientists and other experts in London and Cambridge. At the age of thirty, in 1839, he married his cousin, Emma Wedgwood; it was an exceptionally happy marriage, and the couple remained quietly devoted to each other for the next forty years, until Charles's death.

Like many Victorian couples, they bred a large family: ten children, two of whom died in infancy, and one who died at the age of ten. Darwin, a keen student of the principles of heredity, often worried that he had done his children a disservice by marrying so close a relative, and exposing them to the risks of growing up weak and sickly; though marrying cousins was fairly common (and widely approved of) in wealthy or aristocratic families during the nineteenth century, and this seldom seems to have done much damage to the offspring.

The intrepid world traveler and adventurer had become a cautious stay-at-home and, for about a third of his remaining days, an invalid. Visitors to his home, Down House, often commented on how he had it meticulously and ingeniously arranged so as to facilitate his studies. It was, they said, as if he had deliberately made it into a kind of land-bound *Beagle*.

Biographers are often tempted to use biological metaphors when they write of Darwin's middle and later years.

Since he devoted almost a decade to the dissection and intense study of barnacles – this humble creature proved central to confirming his theories – he has sometimes been compared to a barnacle himself, clinging to his modest plot of land as tenaciously as a barnacle does to a ship's hull. And since a very great deal of his work relied on the increasingly excellent postal services both in Britain and around the globe, and on the rapidly expanding railway networks of the day, he has been compared to a giant spider at the center of a world-wide web. He bombarded his correspondents with queries, and received not only detailed replies but tons of biological and geological specimens to examine.

His account of the voyage of the *Beagle*, originally published in the same volume as Captain FitzRoy's narrative, proved so popular with the general readership that it was issued as a separate volume, and went through several editions. Not that Darwin needed sales to support his family: Dr Darwin funded him generously, and Charles proved to be every bit as shrewd an investor as his father had been. He took pride in the detail and accuracy of his account books; at times, he seemed to derive more contentment from his financial skills than from his fame as a scientist. The same railways that brought him specimens also brought him a handsome income. His donations of specimens to museums and zoos, and the weighty volumes on geology, botany, palaeontology and biology that others developed from his notes won him the highest respect from his fellow scientists. By the time of his marriage he was already acknowledged as one of Europe's leading naturalists.

That was the public man. In private, Darwin had been brooding on the implications of the various enigmas he had discovered in his travels. Gradually, it dawned on him that this random assembly of natural puzzles was showing a clear pattern. In 1838 he read the sixth edition of Malthus's classic *Essay on the Principle of Population*, which showed, among other things, that species, left unchecked, would multiply beyond the capacity of their environment to feed them. (Darwin and Emma had, of course, had personal reasons for brooding on population increase.) Catastrophes and extinctions were an inevitable fact of life.

At the same time, Darwin became interested in the practice of selective breeding, whereby farmers, race-horses trainers and other men who worked with animals would mate their beasts so as to enhance desirable characteristics and eliminate weaknesses. Perhaps if one married the brutal insights of Malthus to the successful breeding methods of pigeon trainers …?

Darwin essentially thought out his fundamental theories about the mutability of species as early as 1839, around the time of his marriage. He contemplated the things he had witnessed in his five years of travel. The oddity of life on the Galapagos, where each island had distinct species of finches and other creatures. The wildlife of Australia, which had tempted him to speculate about different parts of the earth having more than one Creator. The discovery of marine fossils in the sides of a cliff far above sea level. The all but overnight mass destruction of cattle and horses by drought. The astonishing experience of earthquakes and volcanoes, which showed that the earth had not outgrown its days of violent upheaval. The ugliness and poverty of the natives of Tierra del Fuego, and the beauty and contentment of the Tahitians …

He grew increasingly confident in his conviction that there was a connection between all these disparate things. He had learned from his most inspirational teachers that science was largely a matter of accumulating a vast mound of facts, and then formulating hypotheses that would make those facts intelligible. All of his notebooks, all of his specimens, and all of his contemplations were ramming home one inescapable fact. Species had not remained constant since the dawn of Creation. Species change.

Species change. His grandfather Erasmus had been right (but for the wrong reasons), Lamark had been right (for different wrong reasons), and all the evolutionary theorists had been right. Darwin is often loosely said to have "discovered" evolution, but this is far from the truth. Darwin's astounding accomplishment was to discover not evolution itself, but the processes by which evolution takes place and can be shown to have taken place.

Throughout his life, Darwin struggled to come up with a verbal formula that would encapsulate his idea most neatly. The well-known phrase "survival of the fittest" – actually coined by the philosopher Herbert Spencer, though Darwin adopted it, with some reluctance, in his later writing – is dangerously close to a tautology, as his critics were quick to point out in mocking tones. "So, Mr Darwin, you say that it is the fittest creatures that survive?" "Why, yes!" "And how do you know they are the fittest?" "Why, because they have survived ..."

He settled on what seemed to be a neutral term, "natural selection", and continued to use it even after it was pointed out to him by his allies that the metaphor of selection implies a Selector; and Darwin's fundamental insight was that no one, nothing, was selecting anything. His earliest working hypothesis was beautifully simple. Species change, often in response to a dramatic or gradual mutation in the place where they live. (There are other causes of evolutionary change, as he later realized.)

Wetlands become deserts, deserts flood, the sea level rises and falls, land masses are split apart. The plants and beasts that happen to thrive in changed circumstances not only live on, but breed with, their fellow survivors. Offspring tend to take after their parents, so that over time the accidentally useful traits become established. *Species change.*

At heart this is a very simple idea – some consider it beautiful in its simplicity – and it explained vastly more about the nature of life than any previous account, religious or scientific, had been able to. Darwin was almost certain that it was right, but, as noted, he wanted to gather together irrefutable evidence in support of his daring hypothesis – evidence in such quantities that no person of intellectual honesty could avoid concluding that the Darwinian hypothesis had almost limitless explanatory power. That the hypothesis had some points of weakness Darwin never denied. He did not live long enough to see the new science of genetics develop to the point at which, in the twentieth century, it could offer an overpowering corroboration. In 1839 he set out a swift "pencil sketch" of natural selection; in 1842, he expanded it into a 230-page essay. But he did not publish it. As he half-joked to a scientific colleague: "It is like confessing a murder." And the murder victim was God.

For the greater part of two decades, Darwin published on other, less incendiary matters and burnished his reputation. On evolution he kept entirely silent, save amongst a small circle of trusted colleagues. He did not even discuss it much with his beloved wife Emma, since she remained a devout Christian while Darwin inevitably found himself drifting towards atheism – or, to use a word later coined by his friend and champion Thomas Huxley, agnosticism. He ceased to be a believing Christian by about the age of forty.

Darwin maintained this careful silence until, for the second time in his life, an unexpected letter changed the course of his career. It arrived on 18th June 1858, and came from an obscure, self-taught young naturalist named Alfred Wallace, who quite independently of Darwin had been brought to all but identical insights about the significance of natural selection in the development of life on earth. This was an immense shock to Darwin, who feared that Wallace would publish before he did, and that he would appear merely to be riding on the coat-tails of a younger, more brilliant man. Twenty years of hard work would have been made redundant at a stroke. He was despondent, but his ethical principles were so strong that he knew he would have to concede that another scientist had traveled an independent path to the same conclusions. Wallace's insights must be formally acknowledged. It would not be gentlemanly to do otherwise.

Following the advice of his friends, but without consulting Wallace, he arranged for a paper outlining the basics of the overlapping evolutionary theories to be delivered at The Linnaean Society in London, on 1st July 1858; the all but unknown Wallace had equal billing with the distinguished Darwin. Ill as usual, Darwin stayed in Kent; Wallace was still in Malaysia. It was something of an anticlimax; the audience for the presentation did not seem to grasp the shattering implications of this new theory, and it was met with nothing more than mild, indifferent applause. But it had happy consequences. Darwin had been afraid that when Wallace heard about the lecture he would be angry about being upstaged. On the contrary: Wallace sensibly recognized that it might well have taken years for someone like himself – neither a formally educated man nor a gentleman – to have gained any attention from the scientific establishment. Wallace was grateful, and Darwin relieved. In the years ahead, they became warm friends.

Now that the dangerous idea had been made public, even if the limited public did not yet seem greatly interested, it was high time to show in detail how Darwin and Wallace had arrived at it. Writing at what was for him great speed – he found writing difficult, and once said that he would respect anyone who had written a book, no matter how poor it might be – he composed the chapters of the volume that eventually became known, after many abortive attempts at finding a better title, as *The Origin of Species*. It was published on 22nd November 1859, and, to the surprise of both its author and its publisher, its first imprint of 1,250 copies sold out that very day. The savants of the Linnaean Society may not have been much impressed, but evidently a lot of other people were eager to hear this new explanation.

And a great many were not. Attacks came from hostile fellow scientists, from scandalized churchmen, and – as in the notorious public debate in which one of Darwin's rivals had briefed his mouthpiece (none too well) – from scientists using clergyman as their ventriloquists' dolls. Word had got out that Darwin was claiming that humans were descended from apes, a comic distortion which prompted the Bishop of Oxford, Samuel Wilberforce, to enquire of his opponent at a debate in 1860 whether he was related to apes on his mother's or his father's side of the family. It was not much of a joke, and it received the retort it deserved. Wilberforce's opponent was Huxley, who said that he would much sooner be related to an ape than use his authority to make a mockery of science. As so often, both sides of the debate left thinking that their views had carried the day. One of the men present at that meeting was Darwin's former Captain, FitzRoy, who had become more and more passionate in his Christian faith and was dismayed that the voyage of the *Beagle* had been the source of his shipmate's dangerous blasphemies. A few years later, FitzRoy showed how right he had been to fear the precarious states of depression that might bring him to suicide. One morning, he walked into his bathroom and slit his throat.

In the small world of science, it was clear in a matter of months that Darwin's side had won the war, furious as the opposition had been. In 1864, almost five years to the day since the publication of *Origin of Species*, Britain's most powerful and distinguished scientific body, the Royal Society, gave Darwin its highest honor: the Copley Medal. A seal of approval such as this could hardly be ignored by the great and the good.

Slowly, Darwin's health began to improve, and his depressions lifted. He continued to use the grounds of Down House as his practical laboratory, applying himself to two of the subjects which most fascinated him in later life – the propagation of plant life in general and that of orchids in particular, and the huge benefits conferred on mankind by the activities of earthworms. Some of the experiments he carried out on earthworms (and on carnivorous plants – another source of fascination) seemed to outsiders to border on the crackpot, as when he used a bassoon to test their powers of hearing.

Though writing still exhausted him, Darwin published a great deal, including two books that became best-sellers: *The Descent of Man, and Selection in Relation to Sex* (1871) and *The Expression of Emotion in Men and Animals* (1871) – a summary of his intermittent researches which drew on notes he had made as far back as his *Beagle* journeys, and during the infancy of his first-born son. He was mildly bemused to note how warmly these two books were received. The same ideas that had been violently contested a dozen years ago were now considered part of accepted scientific wisdom. He died, serenely, on 19th April 1882. His family wanted him to be buried in their parish church, of which Darwin had been fond, but the politicians and the leader writers of the United Kingdom wanted to show that they knew how to honor a great Englishman. Darwin's funeral was held in Westminster Abbey – no one seemed alive to any irony in this resting place. His body was buried close to that of Sir Isaac Newton.

In his *Autobiography*, Darwin reflected on the fact that his life could have followed a very different course had it not been for the most trifling of occurrences: his uncle Jos's willingness to speak up for the wisdom of his going off on a great adventure, and FitzRoy's willingness to over-look the bad phrenological sign that sat in the middle of young Charles's face. Small matters may have incalculably far-reaching consequences:

> The voyage of the *Beagle* has been by far the most important event in my life and has determined my whole career; yet it depended on so small a circumstance as my uncle offering to drive me 30 miles to Shrewsbury, which few uncles would have done, and on such a trifle as the shape of my nose. I have always felt that I owe to the voyage the first real training or education of my mind. I was led to attend closely to several branches of natural history, and thus my powers of observation

were improved, though they were already
fairly developed ...

I discovered, though unconsciously and
insensibly, that the pleasure of observing
and reasoning was a much higher one
than that of skill and sport. The primeval
instincts of the barbarian slowly yielded to
the acquired tastes of the civilized man.

Had he stayed in England, Darwin's life would very likely
have been like that of his cousin. He would have taken
holy orders, married, raised a large family and used the
considerable amount of free time enjoyed by rural clerics
to pursue his interests in botany. He might have become
a naturalist of some distinction. But it is highly unlikely
that he would have been a pioneer, a scientific revolutionary, a hero. Another scientist – Wallace, probably, or if
not him, Huxley – would sooner or later have published a
work on natural selection, taken the ridicule and then the
praise, and dominated nineteenth-century science.

The simple truth is that his years on the *Beagle* changed
him from Charles the affable idler to Darwin the scientific
genius. It forced him, so to speak, to evolve.

Mayflower: The Voyage from Hell

Kevin Jackson looks at the reality behind the mythic status of the Mayflower – and the journey that 'created' the New World. Most of the voyagers of that famed 1620 crossing of the Atlantic were not in fact religious pilgrims, but people intent on forging a better life for themselves in the virgin territory of America's east coast. 130 hardy souls were confined in a space no bigger than a tennis court, braving the 'Northern' crossing, without any firm idea of what awaited them in the New World. A riveting account of the sailing that changed the world.

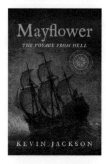

The Queen's Pirate: Sir Francis Drake & the Golden Hind

The Queen's Pirate: Sir Francis Drake & the Golden Hind tells the extraordinary story of Drake's early years and his journey around the world on his famous ship, the Golden Hind. For more than four centuries, Drake has been world-famous for his feats as a master mariner – the captain who "singed the King of Spain's beard" with his daredevil attack on the fleet at Cadiz, and who led the British Navy to victory against the Spanish Armada in 1588. But Drake's exploits in his earlier years, though less well

known, are even more remarkable. Born into a poor, obscure family, he worked his way rapidly up in the maritime world to his first captaincy. Before long, he was the most successful of all English pirates, admired by his countrymen, hated and feared by the Spanish. Queen Elizabeth saw the potential in this rough-mannered but enterprising young man, and gave him her blessing for the first British venture into the Pacific Ocean. This success of this voyage, which lasted for three years, exceeded their wildest hopes. Not only did Drake come home with a vast treasure of captured gold, silver and jewels; he became the first man ever to circumnavigate the globe in a single mission, and bring most of his crew home alive and well.

Also launching soon in the *Seven Ships Maritime History* series: Nelson's *Victory*, Cooke's *Endeavour*, Shackleton's *Endurance* and Bligh's *Bounty*. All available directly, including signed copies, from the publisher at: www.canofworms.net